LIFE
and ART

LIFE
and ART

ESSAYS

Richard Russo

ALFRED A. KNOPF
New York
2025

A BORZOI BOOK
FIRST HARDCOVER EDITION PUBLISHED BY
ALFRED A. KNOPF 2025

Published by Alfred A. Knopf, a division of Penguin Random House LLC, 1745 Broadway, New York, NY 10019.

Knopf, Borzoi Books, and the colophon are registered trademarks of Penguin Random House LLC.

Several essays first appeared in the following publications: "The Future" first appeared in the *Journal of the American Psychoanalytic Association;* "The Lives of Others" first appeared in *Harper's Magazine;* "Marriage Story" first appeared in *Scribd* and *America* Magazine; "Stiff Neck" first appeared in *The Atlantic;* and "Triage" was originally published as a Vintage Shorts Nonfiction Original.

Grateful acknowledgment is made to the following for permission to reprint song lyrics: *BMG*: excerpt from "We Can't Make It Here Anymore" by James McMurtry. Short Trip Music (BMI) administered by BMG. Featured on James McMurtry's album, *Childish Things* (Lightning Rod Records); and *Wixen Music Publishing*: excerpt from "Pancho and Lefty" by Townes Van Zandt. © 1972 JTVZ Music (ASCAP), Will Van Zandt Publishing (ASCAP), Katie Bell Music (ASCAP) admin. by Wixen Music Publishing, Inc. All rights reserved. Used by permission.

Library of Congress Cataloging-in-Publication Data
Name: Russo, Richard, [date] author.
Title: Life and art : essays / Richard Russo.
Description: First edition. | New York : Alfred A. Knopf, 2025.
Identifiers: LCCN 2024022828 (print) | LCCN 2024022829 (ebook) |
ISBN 9780593802168 (hardcover) | ISBN 9780593802175 (ebook)
Subjects: LCGFT: Essays.
Classification: LCC PS3568.U812 L54 2025 (print) | LCC PS3568.U812 (ebook) |
DDC 814/.54—dc23/eng/20240828
LC record available at https://lccn.loc.gov/2024022828
LC ebook record available at https://lccn.loc.gov/2024022829

penguinrandomhouse.com | aaknopf.com

Printed in the United States of America
10   9   8   7   6   5   4   3   2   1

The authorized representative in the EU for product safety and compliance is Penguin Random House Ireland, Morrison Chambers, 32 Nassau Street, Dublin D02 YH68, Ireland, https://eu-contact.penguin.ie.

Contents

Part I

LIFE

Stiff Neck

The call is one we've been expecting, so when it comes we're jolted but not surprised. It's from my wife's sister, who lives in Arizona. She and her husband are both proudly unvaccinated—predictably enough, since their chief sources of information are Fox News and social media. They've believed from the beginning that the coronavirus has been overblown by mainstream media and that doctors are in on it because they somehow get paid more when they record the death of somebody who died in, say, a car accident as having been caused by COVID-19, though how exactly that would work my relatives don't explain. For them, the vaccines are not about public health so much as personal freedom. My body, my choice, and they've made theirs.

And now, the reckoning. For a year and a half they've been lucky, but their luck has finally run out. Both have been infected with the virus. On the phone my sister-in-law can't stop coughing, though she says her own case is relatively mild. Her husband, however, is being put on a ventilator; his chances of survival, according to his doctors, are roughly fifty-fifty. She's distraught, and the question she wants my wife to help her with isn't *How could we have been so stupid?* but rather *Why is this happening?* and she asks this in all sincerity. The obvious answer is one she can't or won't accept—in part, I suspect, because it naturally leads to another question that, even in this excruciating moment, she refuses to entertain: *What else have we been wrong about?*

I can't listen. As my wife tries her best to console her sister, I have to leave the room. The events of the last two years— political, cultural, epidemiological—have seriously eroded my ability to sympathize with people who should damn well know better. I ought to be able to summon a more sympathetic response than *What on earth did you expect?* but often I just can't. I am fed up and, I admit, no longer my best self. Somehow it has come to this. We are now a nation that has to be specifically warned not to drink bleach. Out of necessity, a feedstore owner in Nevada is refusing to sell ivermectin to anyone who can't prove they own a horse. Though three different vaccines against the coronavirus have been proven safe and effective for use here in the United States, and though those vaccines are free, people like my wife's sister and her husband will use up precious oxygen berating their doctors for refusing to treat them as a veterinarian would treat a barnyard animal suffering from a completely unrelated malady. Such lunacy makes common decency difficult to summon and act upon.

When my wife finally hangs up in the next room, I hear her let out a cry of pure exasperation, and for some reason when she does, a memory of my father lurches unbidden from the back of my mind to the front.

WHEN I ENTER the tavern, he's seated at the bar, surrounded by his cronies, one of whom notices my entrance and alerts him. *Jimmy. Your kid.* This is how it's been since I actually was a kid. After my parents separated, I didn't see much of him, but every now and then there he'd be, big as life, talking with some guys in front of the pool hall or drinking coffee at the counter of the Palace Diner. Seeing me approach, somebody would nudge him and stage-whisper, *Jimmy. Isn't that your son?* But that was then. At the time of this particular memory, I'm probably thirty, a newly minted college professor with a recent PhD, and because my life is elsewhere now, I haven't seen him in some time. He has an apartment, of course, a place where he goes to crash after last call, where he showers in the morning and again after work before heading to whatever blue-collar dive bar he and his buddies are gracing these days. So this is where I've sought him out. On a barstool he is the personification of elegance, and I expect him to execute his signature move: the stool itself will swivel, but so, too, will his head, a beat quicker, allowing him to locate me before the stool and the rest of his body complete their arc. This time, though, something is off. Both stool and man rotate as if welded together.

When he hands me a bottle of the beer he remembers me drinking years earlier, while we worked road construction together, I imitate his hunched, rigid shoulders and say, "So, what's all this?"

"Nothing," he assures me. "A stiff neck is all."

"Since when?" I ask.

He shrugs. "A while."

I clock the expression on one of his friend's faces. *Fucking Jimmy,* it says. *What're you gonna do?* So, longer than a while, then.

"It's no big deal," he assures me. "I know a guy."

.   .   .

TURNS OUT the guy he knows is a horse trainer in nearby Saratoga Springs who has access to dimethyl sulfoxide (DMSO), an industrial solvent that is easily absorbed into the skin and used, among other things, to reduce inflammation in racehorses. Doctors prescribe medical-grade DMSO to treat bladder inflammation and irritation in humans, as well as joint pain and shingles. But these days DMSO can also be purchased in various strengths in health-food stores. When my father scores his topical-cream version the day after admitting to me that he has a stiff neck, he will not be supervised by a doctor or even, for that matter, the horse trainer. He's probably been warned not to get it in his eyes if he can help it because, yeah, it's an industrial solvent. But hey, guess what? The stuff actually works! Almost immediately he can move his neck—not a lot, but still. Okay, there are some side effects. It stinks to high heaven. As advertised, it absorbs right into the skin, and from there it keeps on going. My father can taste it, metallic, on the back of his tongue, and because the taste is even worse than the smell, his appetite is pretty well shot. But so what? He isn't going to be using it forever, just until the stiff neck goes away, so he considers the trade-off a pretty good one. By the end of the week, he's his old self, on barstools and off. He considers himself fortunate to know a guy with access to a miracle cure, whereas other people with a stiff neck just have to suffer through it.

You know how this story ends, right? Months later, after a long-deferred trip to the VA hospital, my father will learn that the cause of his stiff neck, which kept returning despite repeated applications of DMSO, is lung cancer. It's a shame he didn't come in sooner, he will be told. Too bad he's wasted precious months treating his lung cancer with horse liniment, which alleviates his discomfort just enough for him to continue working, which even at sixty he still needs to do.

Yes, too bad.

ONE OF THE PROBLEMS with screaming *How could you be so stupid?* at people who behave stupidly is that we too often think of the question as rhetorical when it isn't. Though vaccine hesitancy is often seen as purely political, that's not always the case. It also correlates to lack of health care, which means that when public-health officials urge the unvaccinated to consult their family doctors (on the assumption that they might be more persuasive than government agencies), they're assuming facts not in evidence. If you can't afford health insurance, you probably can't afford a doctor either, and if this is how you've been living for the last decade, chances are good that surviving without sound medical advice has become part of your behavioral DNA. Your strategy will be much like my father's: keep working, save what you can (not much) for the rainy day you know is coming and hope for the best. Maybe you'll get lucky and know a guy.

So, yes, my father was foolish not to go to a doctor sooner, but it's not terribly surprising that he didn't. After he returned from the Second World War, his primary access to health care was the VA hospital, an hour away, in Albany. Road construction in upstate New York was seasonal. Summers, you worked ten-hour days and six-day weeks, so when exactly would you go to the doctor? How would you even know when to schedule an appointment? Winters, when you went on unemployment, you had more time but far less money. You might consult a doctor if you fell seriously ill, but you were unlikely to have a regular physician or get regular checkups. Even if you were injured and in pain, you'd be as likely to turn to somebody on the street to sell you painkillers. (Here again, you'd know a guy.) While unwise, such behavior isn't stupidity so much as lack of resources, and recognizing this should, at the very least, slow our march to judgment.

Okay, you say, but surely there are some things that anybody should know better than to do. Should people really have to be told not to drink bleach? Shouldn't you know better than to refuse a free vaccine whose efficacy and safety have been vouched for by infectious-disease experts, and turn instead to a dewormer vouched for by veterinarians? And when you have a stiff neck, shouldn't you know better than to consult a horse trainer? Maybe, but the irony is that many people who behave foolishly consider themselves to be "in the know," to be in possession of inside knowledge; access to it, for them, is a point of pride. The lesson that life seemed determined to teach my father on a daily basis was that he didn't know anyone worth knowing, that he had no strings to pull. Because he had only a high-school education and worked with his hands, America needed him to understand just how unimportant he was in the larger scheme of things. So the possibility that in this particular instance he actually *did* know somebody worth knowing had to be very rewarding. And to his credit, he didn't want to hoard his good fortune. Like believers in the kinds of conspiracy theories that my wife's sister and her husband routinely devour, my father was anxious to spread the word, to make the introduction, to teach others the secret handshake. *You know Spring Street, right? The gray duplex at the top of the hill? Knock three times. Tell them Jimmy sent you.*

Still, even though you want to spread the word, you don't tell everybody about your guy. You don't tell people who drive expensive foreign cars and have summer homes. They have their own guys, legions of them. No, you only tell people like yourself, people you know on sight by how they dress and carry themselves, by where and what they drink, by the calluses on their hands when you shake. The men of your tribe. Which returns me to the day my father admitted to having that stiff neck. There I was, taking him in as he rotated on his barstool, and marveling, as I often did after not seeing him for a while, at how little he and his world changed over time. His buddies all rolling their eyes when he told me not to worry, that he knew a guy. *Fucking Jimmy. What're you gonna do?* But he was taking me in, as well, which means he knew—he had to know—from my tweed jacket and button-down oxford shirt and loafers and, yes, from my hands, recently grown soft, that I now belonged to a different tribe altogether.

AND YET, how temperamentally alike we were—undaunted by hard work; quick to anger; slow to forgive insults, real or imagined; stubborn beyond belief. We also both delighted in stories, especially lively tales of dim-witted behavior. We both had firsthand, hard-won understanding of foolishness, indeed, idiocy of every stripe. The protagonists of the stories we loved most tended to be guys (some women, too, but mostly guys) who, despite the best of intentions, manage to do the exact wrong thing and at precisely the wrong time, in the kind of setting that guarantees an abundance of witnesses. They aren't stupid, but you wouldn't know it to watch them in action, the way they ignore pertinent evidence, miscalculate the odds of success, head due south and then double down when things start—predictably, though they never predict it—to go terribly wrong. What endears these guys to us, I've always believed, is that we recognize ourselves in their folly. As a novelist, I have just one requirement: I have to be able to imagine myself doing what my characters do, no matter how foolish, because if I would never do that, then they probably wouldn't, either.

By way of illustration, here's a fun fact. Two decades after my father scored his horse liniment, DMSO again appeared on my radar. One Sunday morning in the men's locker room after a racquetball match, I noticed that my opponent, fresh from the shower, was rubbing a clear liquid onto the shoulder he'd injured a month earlier. The stuff stank to high heaven. "What is that?" I asked, and when he handed me the plastic tube, there it was in big red letters: DMSO. It's great for any kind of muscle inflammation, my friend assured me. His only reservation was that you could taste it on the back of your tongue.

Later that same year, when I tore my rotator cuff, I visited the store he told me about, the only one around, he said, that sold this stuff. In fact, they stocked not just the clear-liquid DMSO but also a cream that claimed to be "rose scented." "Lord," my wife said when I emerged from the shower. "What is that god-awful smell?" My shoulder immediately felt better, though, and that evening, to celebrate, I cooked one of our favorite meals. Unfortunately, the metallic taste on the back of my tongue kind of ruined it.

If you Google DMSO, among the first things you'll see is a warning that the product should not be used to treat cancer. Apparently, given its popularity, the warning is necessary.

THOUGH HE KNEW I wanted to be a writer, my father died before I achieved much success, and I often wonder what he would've made of what I do for a living. I suspect he would've seen any connection between his telling stories in bars and my writing them and publishing them as tangential at best. He told stories because they dovetailed so perfectly with drinking beer and watching a ball game on the wall-mounted TV above the bar. To him, *storytelling* was a synonym for slinging some bull, and I often remind myself of this when I read over something I've written and find it pretentious. I'm pretty sure it wouldn't have occurred to my father that what he did for shits and giggles might have a moral dimension. Had he lived, I doubt I ever would have shared with him my conviction that the empathy you need to create characters who live lives different from your own can make you a better person, that it can center and give meaning to your life, the way religion or public service does.

Do I still believe that? I'd like to. But I'd also like to understand how somebody like me, with an admitted soft spot for fools, who actually put the word *fool* in the title of three of his novels, has suddenly and unexpectedly become so utterly fed up with them. By what mechanism does empathy, which has rewarded me so richly as both an artist and a man, morph into knee-jerk hard-heartedness? How exactly did I become a man who wants to scream *What did you expect?* at someone I care for and whose husband is on a ventilator, his life slipping away? That I'm clearly far from alone in my exasperation is cold comfort, as is the distinct possibility that the last few years have taught many of us that there are limits to everything, including, perhaps, basic kindness.

Maybe the time has come to look more carefully at exactly what we're all so fed up with. What if it isn't individual foolishness that we've grown weary of, but rather group folly? Invoking tribalism is reflex these days, but maybe we're missing the tragicomic absurdity of those loyalties. At the end of one of my books, *Straight Man*, a bunch of academics are crowded into a small room (they've been cheering up a colleague who's suffered a cardiac event), and when the time comes to exit, they need to cooperate because the door opens inward. It's no surprise that they're unable to—the whole book has been about their insular squabbling. Against all reason they continue to press forward, en masse. And that's where the book leaves them, trapped in that claustrophobic space. Sure, they'll eventually figure it out and escape, but what they'll never escape, we understand, is themselves and the lives they've chosen.

The book, though readers have found it funny, reflects all too clearly my state of mind when I wrote it. I was, well, fed up—with academic life in general, but most of all with my colleagues, despite how many were friends. The lesson is that rendering judgment on groups of people and their shared behaviors is easier than disapproving of idiosyncratic individuals. Writing off a whole class of people is easier than writing off your brother or father or friend. Which means that maybe I'm not really fed up with my wife's sister and her husband. What I've had it with is the behavior of the tribe they belong to.

And the problem is that tribes are often more than just large gatherings of individuals. They can be greater (or lesser, depending on your definition) than the sum of their parts. For as long as they cohere, they become—some would argue—a whole new organism, like the spontaneous, murderous mob at the end of Nathanael West's *The Day of the Locust*. In appearance, mobs can resemble large flocks of birds that bank left or right at the same instant, as if responding to some unheard command. Clearly, it's what the flock is up to that counts, not the identity of the individual birds. The fact that not everyone who marched on the Capitol on January 6, 2021, meant to take part in an insurrection doesn't really matter. They became part of something larger than themselves and subservient to its will. How? Social media was partly to blame, obviously, its algorithms designed to strengthen the bonds of affinity groups, even if the affinity is criminality or lawlessness. Those same algorithms render us pliable, content to view one another as a "basket of deplorables."

Only after the mob disbands and disperses do we discover in that basket someone we care about. Talk to these people after they've become themselves again, and you discover that, like my father, many were there because they "know a guy" who gave them information that not everybody had. This guy they know probably isn't real in the same sense that the horse trainer who gave my father that DMSO was real. They've never actually met. But by now the deal is familiar to anyone who's online. The guy is selling his product not just to you but to everyone *like* you, and he knows who these people are because you've been so clear about your allegiances. From your "likes" he can deduce your fears, your grievances, your dreams, your social class, your work and life experience. Most of all, he wants you to understand how important you are. Indeed, what needs doing probably can't be done without you. He tells you where to go and what to do when you get there. He lets you in on the secret handshake. *Knock three times. Tell them Jimmy sent you.*

SO, IS THERE hope for us, and for America, or are we witnessing the end of our experiment in democracy? On bad days I'm inclined to believe the latter, because we seem to have been assigned the impossible task of putting the toothpaste back in the tube even as others continue to squeeze it. But maybe that isn't the task at all. Maybe instead of fretting over our collective future we need to recall our individual pasts. Maybe that's why my father paid me a visit when my wife was talking with her sister. Maybe what's important isn't the words her sister was saying on the phone but rather the fact that she called in the first place. Think about it. She knows all too well the tribe my wife and I belong to—educated, liberal, coastal, financially secure. In a word, elite. She and her now-dying husband loathe everything we stand for. We are everything they rail against on social media. Yet, pushed to the brink of despair, it's her big sister, someone she looked up to when they were young, someone who's been a comfort to her through other rough times, that she wants to talk to, someone she imagines might be able to comfort her now. Even though my wife and I don't believe the 2020 election was stolen, or that those who stormed the Capitol were patriots, and even though my sister-in-law keeps hearing that some members of our tribe belong to a pedophile ring that feeds on innocent children and that others of us are hell-bent on curtailing her personal freedoms, she's willing to give my wife a pass.

In this willingness, she's not unlike my father. He, too, was bullheaded, his opinions unshakable. One of his best friends, Calvin, was a Black man, but he remained prejudiced against Black people. All he would say of Calvin, who became Wussy in my novel *The Risk Pool*, was that he was "one of the good ones." Their friendship, so unlikely on the face of it, was as durable as any I've ever known. Maybe my father's bigotry struck Calvin as mostly benign. *Fucking Jimmy. What're you gonna do?* Perhaps most important, they were generous of spirit, not just tolerating each other's foolishness, but reveling in it, a reliable source of shits and giggles.

One warm evening, years after my father's death from lung cancer, Calvin threw open a window of his second-floor apartment and sat down on the ledge to cool off. The way I heard it, he was drinking beer and may have forgotten where he was perched. The story that I tell myself is a bit kinder—that Calvin must've leaned back to laugh, maybe even at some memory of my father, and simply lost his balance. I can easily imagine doing something like that myself.

Fools. Maybe in the end that's the only tribe we all belong to.

Triage

1

I was once asked in an interview, "What's the best thing about being a storyteller?"

"That's easy," I replied. "You get to cheat . . . to live many lives, not just the one you're born to."

"Ah," the interviewer nodded, understanding perfectly. "So, it's the same as reading."

Yes. Exactly. Your interior life, where time and space operate differently. The life in your head, or perhaps your soul, the most private place you have, that you never show in its entirety to anyone. For some, and not without reason, it's a place to steer clear of, and to the extent that you're able to manage that, an inner life can seem almost vestigial. For others, it's a place of strength and solace. For a few—artists in particular—it's the whole point of living.

2

For most Americans, the coronavirus became real in March of 2020, but I will always think of it as beginning earlier, in January, because that's when paralyzing fear unexpectedly entered my life and took up what feels like permanent residence in my psyche. I was in New York City visiting friends and meeting with my publisher when my cell rang at three in the morning, never a good sign. It was my older daughter, Emily. "Dad?" she said, her voice shaking. "Can you come home?"

She was calling from the emergency room at Maine Medical Center in Portland, where her little boy, Henry (then seven), my grandson, was in critical condition. Forty-five minutes earlier he had appeared at his parents' bedside demanding his inhaler. He'd taken a blast before going to bed, so it was too soon for another. Groggy with sleep, Emily and her husband, Steve, might've told him to go back to bed, that he could have another hit first thing in the morning. There are times when every parent has to make critical decisions without understanding in the moment that they are, in fact, critical. Probably they were still on high alert because Henry was getting over a case of the flu, no small thing for a kid with asthma. What they didn't know was that while they were asleep, he'd had a violent coughing fit and collapsed a lung. Had they just sent him back to bed, he might have died.

I wasn't the only one who was away at the time. Barbara, my wife, was in Arizona visiting family. My younger daughter, Kate, and her husband, Tom, both of whom also live in Portland, happened to be in New York as well, though they had an early flight home that morning. I was supposed to be in town for a couple more days, but after hanging up with Emily I called the airline and booked the last seat on the same flight Kate and Tom were on, then called Barbara so she could start making arrangements to return home as well. The last thing I tossed into my suitcase before checking out of my hotel was the small plastic bottle of nasal spray I'd set on the nightstand when

I checked in. There's another on my bedside table at home and a spare in the medicine cabinet. Wherever I am, there's always one nearby in case I wake up with clogged nasal passages. Otherwise, I'd have to get dressed and search out an all-night pharmacy. *Whoa,* you're thinking. *Seriously?* Seriously. Perhaps because I watched my grandfather die of emphysema, the idea of death by asphyxiation is enough to send me into blind, flop-sweat panic. That's why I wouldn't dream of going anywhere without nasal spray in my travel kit and why no matter where I am there's always one on the nightstand where I can find it in the dark. The thought of Henry, a child, not being able to breathe and unable to understand why left me weak in the knees with terror.

At four-thirty in the morning there isn't much traffic in Manhattan, and in a matter of minutes my taxi was speeding through the Midtown tunnel. We made it to JFK in record time, but time, as we would all later learn in the pandemic, elongates when mixed with dread. I remember clutching my cell phone the whole way, checking it every few blocks to reassure myself that I hadn't somehow switched the thing off and missed a call from my daughter. Once I boarded my short flight to Portland, the thing would be useless. I tried desperately to banish the thought that by the time I landed my grandson might be dead, but since the beginning of time has any human being ever succeeded in not thinking something that demands to be thought for the simple reason that we can't bear to think it? Time, plenty of it on that taxi ride. Even time to enter into negotiations: *Take me, not him.* Who was I negotiating with? I had no idea. Whoever could deliver.

By the time we arrived in Portland and took another taxi to the hospital, Henry was mostly out of danger, his collapsed lung reinflated. Here's a fun fact, though, for those who have never experienced something like this or have blessedly forgotten what it feels like. When the worst doesn't happen, when you are for some unknown reason spared what happens to the less fortunate, dread is not vanquished by relief, at least not completely. Because our lizard brains are programmed to prepare us for the worst, fear lingers, metastasizes, issues coded warnings. *Okay,* mine said, *this time you were lucky, but guess what? Now I know right where to find you. . . .*

Fear. Is it also part of the inner life that's so important to artists? On the face of it, you'd think so, but I'm not sure. I suspect that fear, like other powerful feelings, even when it's rendered physical (a plastic bottle of nasal spray?), is a gateway drug to the inner life, the thing that starts the conversation. The one that many people, for good reason, try their best to avoid.

3

Fast-forward eighteen long months to August of 2021. Like many others, I have emerged from lockdown chastened but otherwise pretty much unscathed. Thanks to the vaccine I received back in March, I've begun to travel again and to eat indoors at restaurants and with vaccinated friends. What I'd sensed might be coming for me and mine came instead for others. As the pandemic unfolded, there'd been some cause for alarm. Suddenly, all over the world men and women the same age as my wife and me were gasping for breath, like Henry had done with his collapsed lung. The high-rise apartment building where we were hunkered down in Portland was in essence a vertical cruise ship, and sheltering in place there put me in mind of the aristocrats in Poe's "Masque of the Red Death" who foolishly imagined their many-roomed mansion would protect them from the plague that raged outside, only to discover just how egalitarian death was. Not a few pundits in 2020 tried to convince us of this same lesson—that we were all in the same boat.

This, of course, couldn't have been further from the truth. The vessels we occupied were many and varied. Some were crowded, others leaky. Some capsized in the waves; others simply ran aground. The most fortunate took it all in stride. From the balcony of our high-rise, my wife and I watched the harbor below fill with luxury yachts, their Florida owners drawn by less toxic Maine air. Restaurants—many closed except for takeout—delivered right to their moorings. Thanks to a successful writing career, I too was embarrassingly well positioned to shelter in place, and before long I'd fallen into a new routine, getting up early once or twice a week to shop for groceries with other folks my age, our masks and social distancing protecting us better than we knew. Though it hadn't been my intention, I'd somehow become one of the lucky ones who gets to watch the shipwreck from the shore. Sure, we get lashed with the same wind and rain as those on board the ship, but we're not out there among the jagged rocks and crashing waves. Like it or not, our job—my wife's and mine—would be to increase our charitable giving and try not to indulge in any risky behaviors that would, on account of our age, terrify our daughters. I had a novel to write and I would do my job and write it. I even came up with a new mantra to justify being relegated to the sidelines: *If it mattered before, it still does. If it doesn't matter now, it never did.* The truth rankled, though. There was simply no definition of *essential worker* broad enough to include a seventy-one-year-old novelist. I had little choice but to make the best of a good situation.

All too soon it became evident that the disruption we were living through wouldn't be measured in weeks but rather months, or maybe even years, and with this realization something pivoted. For us lucky ones, lockdown had a silver lining. It stripped away life's noise and clutter, allowing us to identify what was truly important and what we could live without. I got my first inkling of this seismic shift when I picked up my monthly planner one morning and went through it page by page—April, May, June, July, August. What I was looking at, I realized, was my old life, all the obligations I'd agreed to because in the moment I couldn't think of a good-enough reason to say no. Conferences. Speaking engagements. A foreign book tour. A lot of a writer's life, if you've been as fortunate as I've been, entails self-promotion. If your publisher is going to work hard on your behalf, as mine always has, you have to work hard in return. Some would argue that the books themselves are that hard work, that they fulfill the writer's duty to his publisher, but I've always felt that if you're given the opportunity (not every writer gets to tour), you're obligated to take your show on the road, especially if you're good at it. Here, though, was a godsend. Just like that, every single commitment wiped away. Just like that, freedom! I'd been waiting for more than a decade, I suddenly understood, for somebody to tell me to go home and stay there, and somebody finally had. Nor could I reasonably be blamed. Striking a gleeful pen through all those obligations brought home to me how exhausted I'd become by them, how long I'd been at it, how little joy bookstore readings and radio interviews brought me anymore, how resentful I'd become for being pulled away from what I needed most in what will likely be my last decade as a productive writer—more time to read and write and, yes, to think. Something else was dawning on me, as well, though it would be later in the pandemic before the thought truly crystallized. Difficult though it was to admit, I'd gotten comfortable. I'd stopped growing.

The same thing had actually happened to me once before,

around the time my novel *Nobody's Fool* was published. It had been optioned for a film, and the project came together very quickly. In twelve short months, filming had begun, and not long after that it began to snow. Nor did it stop until spring, after the film had wrapped. The movie's director, Robert Benton, liked to revise on the fly based on rehearsals, but as the film fell further and further behind as a result of the weather, that became impossible. It was probably a sign of just how desperate the film's producers were that I was asked to lend a hand. Each day I'd be faxed the scenes they planned to shoot the next day, along with a note from Benton telling me what he needed—a trim or two here, a few additional beats there. The most thrilling thing about all this was that at first I had absolutely no idea what I was doing. *Write long*, Benton advised. He'd use what he could and toss what he couldn't. Though I didn't recognize it at the time, I was getting a tutorial in screenwriting, and after a while, I began to get the hang of it, which was exciting, too. The last time I'd learned so much so quickly I'd been in graduate school. Working on that first film led to others, and for the next decade, instead of dividing my time between writing and university teaching, as I had done for so long, I divided it between writing books and movies. *Look at me!* I thought, jazzed and probably a little full of myself. When I least expected to, I'd learned a new trick.

How strange and dispiriting it was to realize that now, in the middle of a pandemic that—*Hey, look at me!*—I'd fallen into the same trap. Somehow, I'd let myself get comfortable doing what I knew how to do and sharing that knowledge with others. It's not that these aren't worthwhile endeavors. They are. The problem is that the more time you spend doing what you know how to do, the more excuses you have to feel satisfied, to convince yourself what you do and know is full and sufficient.

Why dwell on what you've yet to learn, when what you already know is paying such handsome dividends?

4

In fall and winter 2020–21, it seemed as if each new wave of the pandemic was accompanied by corresponding waves of social, political and cultural unrest: the senseless police killings of young Black men and women and the resulting Black Lives Matter protests, Trump's resounding defeat in the election and his refusal to accept it, his attempts to overturn the election, culminating in the insurrection at the Capitol. In fact, there was so much unrest, that our well-earned fear of the virus at times morphed into emotional exhaustion and despondency. In response, I hewed closely to my new mantra (*If it mattered before,* etc., etc.) and wrote two-thirds of a novel, as well as two long essays and a couple short stories, a remarkable output for me. Far more important than the productivity, though, was the fact that filling up blank pages with stories caused the real world to recede, just as it always had. Even in the best of times, job number one for a good storyteller is to get over yourself, to get out of your own way, let the story work its magic. What a gift to discover that the same holds true for the worst of times.

Still, helpful though writing was during those long months of lockdown, it was really reading that saved me. Nor was I alone. Many publishers had record years. My daughter Emily had to close her Portland bookstore to the public, but it continued to prosper thanks to strong online sales and curbside pickup. People read not just more but differently, books on race and social justice flying out the door, along with classics and children's books. Prepandemic my reading had been largely directed. Like so many authors with name recognition, I'm inundated with requests for endorsements from emerging writers and their editors and publicists. I've always taken these requests seriously, having benefited in my own early career from the generosity of writers like Howard Frank Mosher, John Irving and Pat Conroy, a debt that can only be paid forward. Unfortunately, when you do, you too get a reputation for generosity that ensures your burden will grow. There are never fewer than half a dozen advanced reader's editions on my bedside table awaiting—and mostly not receiving—my attention. The upside is that over the years I've discovered dozens of writers whose work I now follow religiously. The downside is that you get pigeonholed as being receptive to a certain type of book. The Russo profile, not surprisingly, is small-town, class-oriented fiction set in the Rust Belt. I probably should be grateful. But for this pigeonholing I'd be sent every debut work of fiction published in the United States (and beyond). Still, it's a bit like what happens when you subscribe to a music-streaming service such as Pandora or Spotify. They want to know what kind of music you like and allow you to respond with a thumbs-up or thumbs-down on the songs they offer. If you give a song a thumbs-down, you won't have to listen to it again, but as the service becomes more confident that it knows you, it becomes less adventurous in its offerings. The more you teach it, the less useful it becomes. The same holds true in publishing. I'm mostly sent books that remind me of me, the one person I don't need to be reminded of. I'm seldom sent books by Black writers, which I think is a shame, though of course I understand. A Black writer with a debut novel needs a blurb from Colson Whitehead or Chimamanda Ngozi Adichie, not some old white dude. Still, though the logic is hard to fault, things sometimes play out unpredictably. Last year I was sent a debut novel by a young Black writer named Nathan Harris, whose *The Sweetness of Water* knocked me sideways, and I'm told my early endorsement was helpful. Not as helpful as being selected for Oprah's Book Club was later, but still.

At any rate, with more time to read during the pandemic, I found myself reading more books by writers who had less need of an endorsement from me, a lot more nonfiction and many more books written by authors whose lived experience is very different from my own. As a result, despite not getting on a plane for eighteen months, I know I'm going to remember the pandemic as a time of both travel and adventure. I went to Ethiopia to fight alongside some fierce women soldiers (Maaza Mengiste's *The Shadow King*); joined the Wobblies and helped to unionize Spokane(Jess Walter's *The Cold Millions*); lived in a Brooklyn housing project (James McBride's *Deacon King Kong*); joined the police academy and became a DC street cop (Rosa Brooks's *Tangled Up in Blue*); clawed my way up the social ladder in contemporary India (Megha Majumdar's *A Burning*); waited tables in the hope of one day becoming a writer (Lily King's *Writers and Lovers*); became addicted to opioids (Eric Eyre's *Death in Mud Lick*); saw my country anew through the eyes of the son of a Pakistani immigrant (Ayad Akhtar's *Homeland Elegies*); hung out with career criminals (Kevin Barry's *Night Boat to Tangier*); became a neuroscientist (Yaa Gyasi's *Transcendent Kingdom*) and a young right-wing Republican congressman (Jessica Anthony's *Enter the Aardvark*). Wait! There's more. Despite suffering a debilitating disease and being confined to a wheelchair, I tracked down a kidnapper (Will Leitch's *How Lucky*); became a twin with a terrible secret (Brit Bennett's *The Vanishing Half*); became a desperate young woman trying to come up with the money to buy the crappy house she and her mother have been renting (Willy Vlautin's *The Night Always Comes*); and got the living crap scared out of me at the tip of Long Island (Rumaan

Alam's *Leave the World Behind*). Nor were my travels entirely geographical. I time traveled back to sixteenth-century Stratford, England, where I lodged with the family of a Latin tutor turned playwright—yes, that one (Maggie O'Farrell's *Hamnet*); then to Victorian England in pursuit of a mermaid (Jess Kidd's *Things in Jars*); journeyed as a convict from London to Australia (Christina Baker Kline's *The Exiles*); then returned home again to share the adventures of an itinerant musician at the end of the Civil War (Paulette Jiles's *Simon the Fiddler*) and took a stirring midfifties cross-country road trip (Amor Towles's *The Lincoln Highway*). And trust me, this was just the tip of my reading iceberg during those eighteen months.

The question begged by this long paragraph, of course, is: *So what?* I happened to be one of those people who found solace and distraction in books. Others binged on Netflix, still others on video games. When we get our old lives back, what will it matter how we survived? Things will be like they were before, right? Maybe. Unless, like me, those eighteen long months in lockdown have changed you, causing you to wonder, even if we could get them back, how satisfying our old lives would be. In order to be truly comfortable in those lives and to derive maximum satisfaction from having them restored, wouldn't we need to be our old selves? What if we're not? What if it's not just our old clothes that don't fit anymore?

5

This past July there was a piece in *The New York Times* that caught my attention. In "There's a Specific Kind of Joy We've Been Missing," Adam Grant, a psychologist, argued that being able to gather again after isolating for so long allowed us to enjoy the "collective effervescence" that comes with large group activities like concerts and sporting events. Emotions, he went on, are not unlike viruses in that they spread easily from person to person, as fear did in the early days of the pandemic. Zoom meetings and FaceTime calls proved poor substitutes for real social interaction, because "peak happiness," he maintained, is a collective, not individual, experience. Studies showed, moreover, that introverts (I assume he would include people like me who'd been waiting for years to be told to go home and stay there) counterintuitively fared worse in lockdown than extroverts, because isolation, which can look attractive to the socially awkward, leads to anxiety, depression and mental illness, all of which spiked during the pandemic. I wonder, though. There can be little doubt the pandemic has indeed caused many people to become more disconnected, but the idea that loneliness and isolation naturally lead to mental illness doesn't square particularly well with my own experience, nor that of many people I know. It may be that out of necessity our lives have been more isolated and disconnected than they were in the beforetimes, but isn't it worth asking if we've become as isolated from our deepest selves as we've become from our fellow human beings? We hear repeatedly that the events of the last eighteen months have revealed that there are two Americas—one rich, one poor; one Black, one white; one red, one blue; one urban, one rural; one educated, one not. Isn't it possible that those same events have also exposed another divide—between those with active, healthy inner lives and those seeking distraction because they don't?

Of all the books I read during the pandemic, the one that has the most to say about solitude, disconnection, loneliness and the importance of a robust inner life is Maggie O'Farrell's *Hamnet*, which takes place, probably not coincidentally, during a plague. Both Agnes, the book's main character, and her playwright husband are deemed strange by others in Stratford because they both live in their heads. Interestingly, they're different not only from the rest of the village but also from each other, which allows O'Farrell to make the case that artists like Agnes's husband are not the only people capable of rich inner lives. It also appears that women pay a bigger price for being "odd" than men do. Agnes's husband's strangeness is written off as mere dreaminess, an unfortunate tendency to abstraction. To his merchant father this simply means that his son will be of little practical use to him in his business or to the world in general. Agnes's "otherness" seems located in her almost-mystical ability to see connections between things that other people miss. She's endlessly curious and deeply observant, especially of the natural world, qualities that turn out to be very practical indeed. She ends up the closest thing to a real doctor in Stratford, though the villagers seem to believe she's some sort of witch. But as I said, until the end of the novel she's as much a mystery to her husband as he is to her. In the book's final, breathtaking scene Agnes goes to see her husband's play (*Hamlet*) and only then glimpses what it's like to be him.

Though Agnes and her husband are the only two people in the village different enough to be noticed and singled out, O'Farrell doesn't appear to suggest that "normal" people are inferior or somehow deficient. Rather, she emphasizes that the impediments to a healthy interior life are both real and not easily overcome. When life is little more than relentless, repetitious chores, most people at the end of a long day are less interested in self-improvement than distraction from the harshness of existence. In sixteenth-century Stratford, it's both easier and more satisfying for the villagers to be suspicious and resentful of Agnes and her playwright husband than to try and understand them. There's nothing in the lived experience of these farmers and tradesmen that would lead them to believe spinning stories in your head or wandering the forest for hours in search of herbs would be rewarding in either the monetary or spiritual sense.

That's still true five centuries later, at least if my own experience is anything to go by. Now, as then, the one absolute prerequisite to a healthy interior life is a belief in both its existence and its importance, and class remains key. While life in modern America may be less grueling and harsh for many than it was in rural sixteenth-century England, living in your head is still something of a luxury. When I was growing up, my mother worked long hours at General Electric in Schenectady, and being a single mom, her workday didn't end when she returned home at night. A dreamer by nature, she still managed to scratch out and fiercely defend a small patch of inner life. Instead of watching television at the end of her long day, as you might expect, she read books that were full of romance and time travel and swashbuckling adventure. She had no interest in books about people whose lives were difficult or disappointing, because her own was difficult and disappointing. Nor did she desire friendships with women living in circumstances similar to her own. They would only remind her of how trapped she was. Her reading was equal parts escape and distraction, and returning from that distraction was often painful.

My father, who'd been part of the Normandy invasion, had little use for reflection, nor was his postwar life of hard physical labor particularly conducive to an active interior life. Distraction in the form of cold beer and a steady stream of bullshit with men like himself was what was called for. He didn't like to be alone and in fact refused to be. Though his life was no easier than my mother's, he had no desire to escape from it. Yesterday didn't matter to him and neither did tomorrow until it arrived.

The problem with such a philosophy is that it so often leads to poor outcomes. It encouraged him to always be present for last call and allowed him to keep smoking, which reduced significantly both the number and quality of his tomorrows.

Most of my career in education was spent in large state universities where I taught composition (which was required), literature (some sort of survey course was mandatory) and creative writing (an elective). Tuition and room and board at these public institutions were relatively inexpensive, but things are expensive if you don't have the money to pay for them, and many of my students' parents were making significant sacrifices to send them to college. They reminded me a lot of my own parents and, yes, of those sixteenth-century villagers in *Hamnet*. Determined to protect their investment and having little or no experience of higher education themselves, they were often resentful of the time and money "wasted" on the classes I taught. I know this because they told me. They were sending their kids to the university because they wanted a better, easier life for them, by which they generally meant one with fewer financial headaches. Many of the fathers, like my own, had not taken advantage of the GI Bill and had witnessed those who did prosper disproportionally as a result; what they were after for their children was job training, not "education" per se, and God help the son or daughter who got turned on by a humanities class and announced over Thanksgiving dinner that they'd decided not to major in business after all but rather philosophy. In other words, what stands in the way of selling the life of the mind to well-intentioned folks like these—now, as in sixteenth-century Stratford—is a toxic mix of ignorance and, yes, love. Having been denied the luxury of reflection themselves, and doubting that it can be monetized, such parents often considered the arts and humanities, as well as many of the social sciences, a waste of time and money. Where is the margin, they wondered, in pondering the meaning of life when we're put here to live it? If asked, they would doubtless agree with Adam Grant (and my father) that life's greatest joys are communal in nature, inextricably connected to work, to sports, to church, to neighborhood, to region, all of which, as many have pointed out, were under stress long before the pandemic. The virus didn't just lock down people like me who for some time had secretly been hoping to be sent home and told to stay there; it also sent into isolation millions of others who'd grown accustomed to a wide variety of distractions that were suddenly no longer available to them. No wonder so many of them disappeared down social media rabbit holes that provided not just community but moral certainty.

6

Writers and other artists come at life differently. Where others want answers and certainty, we're drawn to questions, the more complex and unanswerable the better. We're so obsessed with the meaning of experience that we sometimes stand back and observe others navigating its shoals instead of risking those shoals ourselves. And our work is often solitary. So, if Grant's thesis about solitude and introversion leading to increased anxiety, depression and mental illness were true, you'd think writers and others who live in their heads would be particularly susceptible, doubly so if you subscribe to the notion, as many do, that there's a link between creativity and mental illness to begin with. Indeed, though no such direct link has been borne out by research, there are some fascinating indirect ones. For example, studies have shown that siblings of people who suffer from serious mental disorders often score high on tests for creativity, leading some to speculate that they possess a watered-down, more manageable "variant" (to borrow Grant's virus metaphor for how emotions are transmitted) of their sibling's malady, one that allows them to remain functional, often highly so. I'm pretty sure I've seen this at work on the maternal side of my own family, through which obsessive-compulsive disorder has cut a wide swath. Though never professionally diagnosed, my mother suffered paralyzing panic attacks throughout much of her life, and over time she developed ritualistic behaviors designed to reassure her that she was in some kind of control. As she aged, however, these once-comforting rituals became more aggravated and ascendant until, in the end, like so many OCD sufferers, she became a slave to the very habits she'd invented to keep anxiety at arm's length.

As a boy I, too, was a secret worrier, always on the lookout for trouble, and later I began to exhibit obsessive behaviors of my own, though these seemed to play in my head at a much-lower volume. In my late twenties, when I started writing, I imme-diately became hooked, not because I was talented (I wasn't, particularly), but rather because the activity itself *felt* so good, its necessary rituals—writing every day at the same time and in the same place with the same tools—profoundly satisfying. At the time I didn't recognize the link between my new addic-tion and my mother's ritual behaviors, but I should have. In her apartment every object, each knickknack, had to be positioned perfectly on top of the credenza or the TV or the kitchen coun-tertop. If she sensed that something wasn't quite right, she'd rise from her chair, cross the room, move the offending porcelain ballet dancer a quarter of an inch to the right or left, then go back and sit down again. If it still wasn't right, she'd rise and move it again. Only when she'd convinced herself that everything was exactly where it ought to be—sometimes this would take hours—could she rest easy. I'm no easier to please when I'm revising sentences, which, as I've gotten older, I do more and more obsessively, the difference being that those sentences *do* improve. Getting them to run smoothly is important, both to me and to readers, whereas the exact positioning of that porcelain dancer mattered only to my mother. My point is that the same impulse that was symptomatic of a debilitating mental illness in her, sufficiently diluted in me, turned a liability into a strength.

I can't emphasize enough that none of this has anything whatever to do with moral character. I was simply different enough from my mother and from *her* mother and her mother's sisters to stand a fighting chance. We creative types like to think of ourselves as superior people, but we're not. We do, however, seem to be configured in ways that allow us to achieve something akin to peak happiness in solitude. For us, profound joy is not always a collective experience, as Grant argues it must be. It isn't that we're incapable of "collective effervescence." Far from it. The first thing my wife and I did after we got our second jabs was throw an outdoor party for our vaccinated writer friends and, trust me, we effervesced. What struck me most, though, was that given what we'd all been through, the many months of isolation and dread, we weren't the walking wounded I'd expected. We were humbled by the experience, yes, and more than a little beleaguered, but not terribly damaged. My impression—and I admit it may be no more than an impression—was that we'd done more than just survive. We'd come out of our enforced isolation more acutely attuned to the world around us—somehow more ourselves for the dreadful experience, not less.

7

Nobody's ever asked me what the worst thing about being a storyteller is, so I'll just have to pretend someone did.

It's not the loneliness, though it can be lonely.

It's not the economic precariousness of the endeavor, the lack of a regular paycheck or the all-too-real possibility that whatever you're working on may not pan out, though sometimes it doesn't.

Nor is it the discouragement of not really knowing how to do something you've done many times before and by now bloody well *should* know how to do, though yes, that *is* discouraging.

For me the worst part is the nagging suspicion that in the final analysis, telling stories may not be the moral vocation we like to pretend it is. In *Hamnet*, when Agnes learns that her husband has written a play called *Hamlet*, she is morally outraged. He has *used* their dead son to sell theater tickets. How *dare* he defile the memory of the child Agnes herself continues to mourn long years after his passing? That art might provide comfort, understanding and even growth doesn't occur to her until she sees how her husband has transformed their solitary sorrows into something shared, that shared sorrow lessens their burden by making them less lonely. His motives, she realizes, weren't mercenary at all.

Most days, I too find that argument reassuring. It was years after my mother's death before I allowed myself to write about her life in my memoir, *Elsewhere*, the only one of my books that I didn't tour with because I imagined readers would confront me about being a terrible son. After she struggled her whole life to keep her obsessive-compulsive disorder a secret, I, the person she trusted most in the world, betrayed her. *How dare I!* Later, when I started getting letters from readers who were dealing with some form of mental illness, thanking me for making them feel less alone, I was grateful for their kindness and reassurance. That gratitude soured quickly, though, when many of those same readers complimented me on what a good son I'd been and what a brave book I'd written, because neither of those statements felt particularly true. Why? Maybe because, comforted though I was by *Hamnet*'s ending, Agnes's initial question, so full of moral outrage—How *dare* he?—wasn't, at least for me, completely or satisfactorily answered. Maybe what it comes down to is this: carpenters use hammers and nails, plumbers pipes and wrenches, electricians wires and tape; writers use people. Everyone unlucky enough to cross paths with a writer is fair game, including, perhaps especially, those we love.

To illustrate this point, allow me to return for a moment to that taxi ride from Manhattan to JFK when my grandson was in intensive care. I've described in some detail the stark terror of that journey. I left out one thing, though, and I'm profoundly embarrassed to include it now. There is, I think, in good artists something that allows them to step back and coolly assess experience—any experience—in real time. We triage everything that happens to us, separating what's useful from what isn't. Not what's useful to the world or to humanity, though we hope it will be useful to both. For the artist, two profoundly contradictory impulses can coexist in the same moment. In that taxi, even as I would have willingly traded my life to guarantee the continued existence of my grandson, I also took that step back and did that terrible triage. *Remember this,* my lizard brain advised. *This is good. You can use this later.* In such a moment, I fear, we glimpse how nakedly the act of creation is about ourselves. It's not so different, really, from the moment when you wake up in the middle of the night, terrified, your nasal passages clogged, unable to breathe. Later, when you're able to breathe freely again, everyone and everything you love about your life returns to you, trailing shame for forgetting these, even for a panicked moment. We tell ourselves that we don't deserve to be judged by our worst moments, and that's probably right. In that moment of triage, though, we glimpse something that, once seen, is difficult to forget—the possibility that the inner life we so prize may be, in its essence, utterly amoral.

Meaning

I'm walking, as I do pretty much every day, along the Eastern Promenade near my home in Portland, Maine, when I feel my wedding ring slip off. Luckily, my hands are in my jeans, so no harm done. I slip the ring back on without breaking stride and return to contemplating Casco Bay. I make it another ten yards or so before it happens again. When the ring slips off my finger a third time, I give up and leave it there at the bottom of my pocket. Though the jeans I'm wearing are relatively new, I double-check anyway to make sure there's no hole in the pocket. Having read Tolkien, I know some rings want to be lost, others to be found, and I've already lost one wedding ring, though that was decades ago.

The ring in my pocket doesn't actually *want* anything, of course. It's just a piece of metal and has no meaning other than what I attach to it. It's sliding off my finger because it's January and bitter cold and my skin is dry and—who knows?—maybe I've lost a couple pounds. As I said, it's perfectly secure right where it is, yet here I am fretting about its safety and unable to reconcile its being in my pocket when it belongs on my finger.

My parka has a tiny pocket with a zipper, and I consider putting the ring there, but that would further distance it from the finger it's supposed to be on. Also, the zipped pocket of my parka carries its own risks. I'm seventy-three and my memory is becoming porous. Sometimes I have to page back through whatever novel I'm working on because I can't remember the name of a character who's been absent from the last couple chapters. And like many men my age I too often find myself in front of the open refrigerator, peering at its contents in the hopes of spotting the reason I'm standing there. Am I even in the right place? Is what I'm looking for in the washing machine? The silverware drawer? The pantry? If I put the ring in the pocket of my parka where it can't possibly fall out, will I forget doing so? If so, then two or three years down the road the ring will go with the parka to Goodwill, and in the meantime I'll be left to contemplate what it means that I've managed to lose not one but two wedding rings. To some people—maybe even to me— that might appear subconsciously intentional. My therapist, if I had one, would surely agree, which is why I don't have one.

Part of the reason I'm fretting is that this would be a terrible time to lose the ring. For the last several months my wife has been suffering from headaches that we've been unable to diagnose. MRIs and biopsies seem to have ruled out the most terrifying scenarios, but there's something scary about not knowing, especially in the wake of the pandemic, which reacquainted all of us with mortality and the uncertainty of the future, realities that in the beforetimes we managed to sequester in the back of our brains. To lose my wedding ring at a time when my wife's health is in question would *mean* something, wouldn't it? Yes? No?

.   .   .

OKAY, SO NOW I'm going to tell you another story about this same ring, one you may find difficult, maybe even impossible, to believe.

As I said, my wife and I reside in Portland, but for many years we lived up the coast in Camden, where we bought a large, rambling house. It had been on the market a long time because it was old and needed a lot of work and was located on busy Route 1. The first couple years we were in it we spent a small fortune replacing windows, shoring up the back deck, updating some old knob and tube wiring so the place wouldn't burn down, renovating the impossibly dated kitchen and purchasing new stainless-steel appliances. Money well spent, because our Camden years were wonderful. Our daughters came of age in that house, and when they went off to college and later moved away to begin their own adult lives, Barbara and I threw raucous, wine-soaked dinner parties for our friends, many of whom were also empty nesters. For the first time in my life I was able to write full-time, an unbelievable luxury. Barbara, an office administrator, got in the spirit of things by shifting gears and becoming a realtor. Summers, we had loads of visitors. Okay, life wasn't perfect. (Did I mention the summer visitors?) I was traveling a lot and Camden was two hours from the airport in Portland, but all in all it was a magical decade and a half of good health, freedom from financial anxiety and general well-being, and it is in this happy context that I offer the story that many will disbelieve, in whole or in part.

But here goes. I'm in our renovated kitchen. I've just returned something to the fridge. I'm hurrying because, well, I'm always hurrying, even when there's no reason to. When I close the refrigerator door and head to the sink, I'm simultaneously aware of two things—that my wedding ring is not on my finger and that, just a split second before, it was. Time stops while I wait for the inevitable *plink* of the ring landing on the floor or a countertop. But . . . no *plink*. I examine my ring finger, half expecting to find it there, because, though I *sensed* its absence, I didn't actually feel the ring slip over my knuckle and off my finger, like I would a decade later walking along the Eastern Promenade. But no, the ring is *not* on my finger. It seems impossible that it could be inside the refrigerator, but I check anyway. Maybe when it slipped off my finger, it landed on something soft. A bag of spinach maybe, or a wedge of Brie. But no, it's not in the fridge. I know this for a fact because I take every single thing out and examine the empty shelves.

When my wife returns, she finds me shining a flashlight into the garbage disposal. The ring, I'm theorizing, flew through the air, landed noiselessly on the rubber seal put there by manufacturers to keep dimwits from sticking their fingers into the disposal when it's running, after which the ring slipped, sans *plink*, into the mechanism. Wildly improbable, you say? Maybe, but if you've read Sherlock Holmes, then you know that once all plausible explanations have been ruled out, the only remaining explanation, no matter how far-fetched, must be true. My wife has not read Sherlock Holmes and does not share his logic, and she demonstrates this by turning on the garbage disposal. I wince, fully expecting to hear the sound of my wedding ring being chewed to bits. But again . . . no.

I should be grateful to have been proven not just wrong but borderline lunatic, but I'm not. My wife's explanation for the missing ring makes elegant use of Occam's razor. The ring slipped off my finger earlier in the day, or the day before, or last week, and I've only now noticed its absence. I am, like my father before me, a careless man. Hadn't I admitted as much years before when my first wedding ring went missing? Barbara had wanted to replace it with another gold-plated one,

but I'd talked her out of it. The battleship-gray titanium ring
we settled on instead was attractive but not terribly expensive,
so that when I lost it as well, we wouldn't feel so bad. A failure
of imagination as it turns out, because here I am, staring at
the stainless-steel sink of our remodeled kitchen in Camden,
Maine, feeling really, really bad.

NOW FAST-FORWARD a couple years. During this period my
wife and I have discussed replacing the second ring but somehow haven't gotten around to it. Because, really, what would
be the point? I'd just lose that one, too. And since there's no
remedy for my carelessness, Barbara has had little choice but to
send me out on book tours, to writers' conferences, to the West
Coast to work on film projects, as an apparent bachelor. During this same period our daughters have married and moved
away. One is living in Brooklyn, the other in London. It seems
unlikely they will ever live in Maine again, and with them per-
manently gone Camden has begun to feel remote, our large
house too full of empty rooms. We think about selling the place
and setting up shop in Boston or maybe on the Cape. We've
had a great run in Camden, but all good things come to an end.

What I will miss most is the kitchen, and this is where I
am when the thing you're not going to believe happens. Once
again I'm in a hurry and I go to the refrigerator, where I find
what I'm looking for (back then when I opened the refrigerator
door I knew what I was after), grab it with my right hand and
close the door with my left. And just like that, in the time it takes
to say *Bilbo Baggins,* the missing ring is once again on my finger.
Not instantly. It didn't just materialize. Rather, I felt it magi-
cally slide on. That reality, however, is seriously undermined by
the fact that it *couldn't have,* so when I look down at my hand and

actually see it there, I just about fall on the floor. Where has it been this whole time? In an adjacent dimension? But then, suddenly and blessedly, clarity arrives, and I understand. All this time the ring has been right where I put it. The handle on the fridge, like the one on the freezer, is not rectangular but rather curved, like a human ear—wide at the top, narrow at the bottom. You'd be much more likely to grab it at the top, where there's room for your whole hand, than farther down, at the ear's lobe, where there's barely room for, say, your ring finger. The day I lost the ring, I'd shut the door and without thinking slid my fingers down the handle as I turned toward the sink. My ring had wedged itself into the handle's curved bottom and remained there, patiently awaiting the return of my finger. I'd felt the ring both leave and return as a vague sensation that was difficult to ignore but also impossible to trust. Because come on, what were the odds? How many times—month after month after month—had my wife and I been in and out of that refrigerator? How many times had we slammed the door? How could it have remained there all that time? Answer? *Somehow*. It had *somehow* remained there where I unwittingly put it, not just wedged in but invisible, because you'd have to bend over at the waist to see it, and even then you'd be unlikely to because the stainless-steel handle of the door was the same color as the ring.

So. How much of this story do you believe? None? Some? All? How much *should* you believe? After all, I'm a professional liar. To me, though, whether or not you believe the story is immaterial. My point is that stories, by their very nature, are incubators for meaning. We tell them to entertain but also to make sense of things, or try to. Science would have us believe that very little of this world, or our experience of it, is intrinsically true. No matter how much we might want it to, the world, science argues, doesn't *mean* anything. It simply *is*. Much of what we want to believe may well be an illusion, because in the end we have the same purpose as all other life-forms—to successfully transmit our genes so that the species survives. Our desire to believe otherwise, to attach meaning to experience, is probably linked to our desire for agency. (Granted, not everyone is comforted by the idea of agency; some would be consoled by the lack thereof, because if free will is an illusion, then we're off the hook, blame-wise. Like the world we inhabit, we simply *are*, no need to fret over complicity.) To a storyteller, however, agency is as necessary as the air we breathe, and as natural. I'd no sooner lost my wedding ring than I began to attach meaning to the loss: it was gone because I was and had always been a careless, easily distractible man. Ironically, the ring's return altered that narrative, but its replacement was just as heavily freighted with personal significance; my marriage, as it turned out, was strong enough to withstand the carelessness that I'd feared might doom it. Or maybe the ring's return meant something else entirely. Maybe my wife and I were being given permission, or even encouragement, to leave Camden, to begin the next phase of our lives together. Now here was a meaning I could embrace.

Except it's apparently not the last word on the subject, because a decade into that next and possibly final phase of our lives together, I am once again fretting as I walk along the Eastern Promenade, and not about something new but rather the same old thing. Despite accepting—at least in the rational part of my brain—that the ring in my pocket has no intrinsic meaning, I can't help *feeling* that it does. Rightly or wrongly, I often *sense* that the world is seeking my full attention, as if there's something about my experience that it's afraid I'll miss. Which would explain why, over time, I have developed such a powerful conviction that even if the scientists are right and our lived experience has no intrinsic meaning, we are morally obligated to behave as if the opposite were true, as if divining its meaning were our primary mission.

What's become clear during the writing of this essay—and probably should've been clear from the outset—is that what I've been fretting over all this time was never about the ring itself. It's also clear that the meaning storytellers and other artists delight in searching for is infinitely flexible, tacking and veering with abandon as circumstances on the ground change. Is this a bug or a feature? I'm inclined to believe the latter. We tell ourselves it's answers we're after, but maybe it's the questions we love.

Beans

Al's barbershop, circa 1957. Upstate New York mill town. The sign in the window says HAIRCUTS. NO WAITING. I'm a boy and my father doesn't live with my mother and me, so when I need a haircut it's my grandfather who takes me. The NO WAITING sign troubles me. Every time we go to Al's, the chair is occupied, so we go inside and sit down and wait until it's our turn. I keep expecting the police to come in and point to the sign and tell us we're not allowed to wait. We should stand outside in the cold until the chair is unoccupied. Somehow, time after time, we get away with this clear violation of the rules. Then one day I *understand*, and this, in a nutshell, is my life as a boy in our small town: I don't understand until, suddenly, I do. I learn not to ask questions, because, in the fullness of time, all will be revealed.

Eventually, I'm allowed to go to Al's without my grandfather. Al is Italian, as in from the old country. Not like my absent father, who's American and, I'm told, a war hero. (That he could be both a war hero and absent is another thing that confuses me, but I have faith that one day I'll understand.) Al is a talker. He likes to make conversation, even with boys my age. "What are you having for dinner tonight?" he wants to know as he snips. I tell him I'm not sure. My mother works at GE in Schenectady, so whatever my grandmother is fixing. Pork chops? Chicken noodle soup? I offer him a range of possibilities. Al invariably says that he and his wife will be having *pasta fagioli*. Every single time he says this, what I hear is *pasta fah-zool*.

When I mention this exotic dish to my mother, she tells me I wouldn't like it. She explains that it's foreign, immigrant food made from cheap ingredients, like macaroni and beans and olive oil. Americans don't eat food of this sort. They eat meat and cook with butter, not oil. Confused, I tell her that Al is always nice to me and he seems to look forward to his *pasta fah-zool*. My mother admits that, yes, Al is a nice man, but claims that he's not like us, which confuses me even more because my absent father is also Italian. And what am I to do with the other obvious similarities between Al and our own family? Each year, as fall segues into winter, my grandfather rubs his hands with glee, anticipating the return of his favorite meal: baked beans and brown bread, both from the can. Not Campbell's, which does offer canned beans, but the far-superior B&M brick oven brand. They remind my grandfather of Vermont, where he's from. He tells me the reason we don't eat them all year round is that it's too hot in the summer. The oven would overheat our small kitchen. In winter, though, if he had his way, we'd eat them every single night. Though I've never known my grandfather to lie to me, I suspect that this is not entirely true, because who would want to eat the same thing every night? Also, while baked-bean season does dovetail nicely with cold weather, when a warm kitchen is comforting, it also coincides, in our town, with the men who work at the tanneries and glove shops getting laid off and going on unemployment until spring.

In anticipation of this annual recurrence, my grandmother dutifully stocks the pantry with canned beans—green, waxed, B&M baked—throughout the summer. Beans are inexpensive, and they get us through the winter until my grandfather has a regular paycheck again. So, I suspect that Al and my grandfather are more alike than my mother is willing to admit: they've both decided to love what they can afford. So, what's really wrong with *pasta fah-zool?* Maybe in time I will understand.

Now, fast-forward thirty years. (That should be time enough.) My wife and I now live in Maine, where I teach and write. We've rented a small apartment in Venice, Italy, for two weeks. We hear that a couple we're friends with on the coast of Maine, both teachers, will be shepherding a group of high-school students around the city, so we make plans, well ahead of their arrival, to have lunch at a favorite restaurant of theirs and ours, Ristorante alla Madonna. The night before, I feel like I'm coming down with something and, sure enough, the next morning I wake up with a sore throat. By lunchtime, that throat is actually closing. I'd hoped to order my favorite dish, spaghetti with squid ink and cuttlefish, but by the time we arrive at the restaurant, I know I'll never be able to swallow the cuttlefish, which in texture resembles calamari rings. In fact, I'm not sure I'll be able to eat anything solid, so when we're seated, I scour the menu for soups, and there it is: *pasta fagioli.* When it comes, I begin to feel relief even before the first spoonful reaches my lips. The soup's aroma isn't just rich; it's heady, and that first spoonful glides down my ruined esophagus like warm silk. Does my throat actually begin to open up? I don't know. Probably not. But I remember Al all those years ago trying to sell me on the merits of his wife's *pasta fah-zool,* as well as my mother tenaciously trying to dissuade me. She, I realize with shame, had triumphed. In the forty years since

Al recommended it, I've eaten every other Italian dish under the sun: calf's liver, scungilli, various sweetbreads and viscera, even tripe. But until that day I avoided *pasta fagioli* because my mother told me—and I believed her—that I wouldn't like it, that people who ate such food were not like us.

These days, I'm an adventurous eater, not at all averse to sucking the brains out of a prawn. And much of what confused me as a boy has, in fact, been made clear. At seventy-two, I mostly adhere to my old conviction that what baffles me today will become clear tomorrow. I now understand how a man can be both a war hero and also largely absent from his own son's life. In many respects, my stubborn faith that I'll eventually get to the bottom of things is fundamental to my being a novelist, because every time I start a new book, what I *don't* know dwarfs what little I do know. And yet I suspect that maybe I need to start asking more questions. Time, after all, is running out, and while it may be true that answers have a way of presenting themselves, even to unasked questions, too much of importance remains shrouded in mystery and paradox. Like this: I love good food and am excited by new dining experiences, many of which are expensive. It's no accident that the best of what life has to offer is seldom cheap. But I'm also suspicious of anything fussy or that needlessly (to my mind) pushes the boundaries of expense. I'd like to think this is not because *I'm* cheap. In fact, I fear my wife and I spend far too much money on food. But I won't order a sixty-dollar steak, even if someone else is paying for it, because there isn't enough béarnaise sauce to mask the taste of shame that eating a sixty-dollar steak would occasion. Indeed, that shame would yank me right out of the fancy restaurant, as well as the present moment, and plop me back down in my grandmother's kitchen, the pantry of which was full of what the people I loved as a boy could afford. What my grand-father and Al the barber were both trying to teach me, it seems, is to love what you're given by the people who mean the most to you. If it's the best they have to offer—and it was—then there's nothing better. There's mystery in that. And maybe wisdom.

Marriage Story

1

I was a boy when my parents separated but an adult before I began to comprehend fully what their separation was about, just how many moving parts there actually were. In the beginning my mother was my only source of information, and I had little choice but to accept what she told me as true. Nor did she lie to me. She just did what storytellers do to control their narrative: decide where to begin the story she wanted me—her audience—to hear, decide what to emphasize, what to downplay as unimportant, what to leave out entirely. She admitted there were things she couldn't share with me yet, that I was being told what I could wrap my young mind around, and I accepted this explanation. Still, the facts were pretty damning to my father. He was, she explained, a compulsive gambler, and he was losing money we needed to live on. Sometimes, when the phone rang late at night, the callers were not very nice men that my father owed money to, demanding to be paid back. When I asked why my father didn't just stop gambling, she explained that he wanted to, but he couldn't. He had what was called an addiction, and that was why he wouldn't be living with us anymore. Was this forever? I wanted to know. Well, that was up to him.

It was a simple, clear narrative and, in its broad strokes, true. Over time, though, the story would expand, like a dry sponge in water. It would come out that their separation wasn't just about my father's gambling. He had also disappointed my mother in other ways. She felt, in a word, cheated. As she saw it, when my father returned from the war, things were supposed to go a certain way, and that wasn't how they were going. After a year or two of celebrating victory, most everyone my mother knew was settling down, starting families, buying homes or going back to school on the GI Bill. In short, getting on with life. But as others moved forward, she and my father stalled, and by the time I came along the writing was on the wall. In this way I came gradually to understand that there was such a thing as context and that it had a way of revealing just how inadequate naked facts are to true understanding.

For instance, my father wasn't the only gambler in town. In fact, most of Gloversville, the upstate mill town where we lived, was to one degree or another addicted. Our proximity to Saratoga Springs was part of it. This was before offtrack betting, but just about everybody played the horses. Every blue-collar bar in town had a bookie installed in a booth or at the end of the bar to take small daily-double wagers, as well as bets on the daily number. These same bookies also circulated in the glove shops and tanneries during the workday. They didn't need to sneak in, either. Though it was never said out loud, they were there with the blessing of the shop owners and the job foremen. Leather was the only business in town, and as a result wages were depressed. Gambling helped keep workers poor and in line, a small price to pay for a tiny decrease in worker productivity.

Still, if horse racing and betting the daily number had been the only wagering in town, all might have been well. For my father, the real problem was the poker rooms above the pool hall where he sometimes worked as a dealer. There players tipped dealers for winning hands, which could be lucrative, provided you remained on that side of the table. My father often didn't. When he finished a shift, he would take his earnings next door or down the hall, where another game was in progress, often for higher stakes. It was here that he racked up the debts that so terrified my mother. How large were they? Was it hundreds of dollars he was losing? Thousands? I never learned the details, maybe because my mother didn't know herself. Nor was it entirely clear to me whether it was the amount of the debt that frightened her or the behavior itself, the fact that the man she was married to, a man she thought she knew, was out of control and keeping secrets from her. When she tried to pin him down about the extent of his losses, he lied. That my father was in over his head was pretty clear, even to him. Sometimes when he got in too deep he'd just blow town, visit a friend downstate where he could stay out of trouble for a while, let the craving diminish, maybe make a little money to pay down his debt. He always returned, though, to Gloversville, to his friends and family, each time with a fresh resolve to stay out of the poker rooms, though he always drifted back there in the end, and the cycle would repeat. He was ill, my mother reminded me. He wasn't a bad man, just a sick one.

If so, he had company. Though she would never admit it, my mother was ill, too. As a boy this was something I both knew and didn't know. I saw the illness in her erratic behavior, as well as in the worried glances of my grandparents, whose house we shared. That something was seriously amiss was obscured by the fact that my mother held down a coveted job at General Electric in Schenectady, where she made a better salary than my grandfather, a glove cutter, and most of the other men who worked in the town's skin mills doing jobs that were not just mind-numbingly repetitious but also dangerous and even toxic. That she worked at GE was for my mother a point of great pride, and she particularly enjoyed comparing the "real" job she had there with the work other local women did sewing gloves at home, piecework that paid even less than their husbands made in the shops.

Even better, when she went to work, my mother got to dress up. A stylish, attractive woman, she much preferred the company of men to that of women, and though it galled her to make considerably less money than men doing the same job because they had families to support, she was proud of holding her own in a man's world, of being responsible not only for herself but for her son, proud of the independence that working for a big, important outfit like GE afforded her. What no one outside the family suspected was that my mother's prized independence was at least in part a fiction. It was my grandparents who originally purchased the house we shared so that, when my parents broke up, she and I would have a place to live, and the rent she paid them for our upstairs flat was below market value. And, of course, to be truly independent she'd have had to pay for childcare, which my grandmother provided for free. When I came home from school, it was she who met me at the door, not my mother, and on weeknights I ate dinner with her and my grandfather, so that my mother could just toss a frozen dinner in the oven when she got home from work.

None of this is intended to diminish my mother's truly heroic efforts on our behalf but rather to suggest that the approved narrative of our lives, which I suspected my grandparents were not permitted to contradict, came at a cost. I wouldn't understand until I was an adult that the story she told herself about our lives buoyed her up when things were going well, but turned on her viciously when they weren't. She could boast all she wanted about her independence, but deep down she had to know the truth, that not only was she being subsidized but that even with this subsidy she was still balancing on an economic knife edge. Worse, she was putting my grandparents, who themselves had little financial cushion, at risk as well. Each month she budgeted down to the penny, praying that nothing unexpected would come up. When something did, her eyes would go wild with terror and her hands would begin to shake. Rather than allow me to see her in this condition, she would retreat to her bedroom, closing the door behind her, and there she would stay, often for hours on end, until she was able to compose herself. When she finally emerged, she would sit at the kitchen table with a cup of coffee, her head in her hands. When the coffee grew cold, she'd rise, go downstairs and ask my grandparents for another loan, explaining why she needed the money and promising to pay them back. By cutting corners and doing without, she always managed to, but having to ask in the first place was not just profoundly humiliating but also an admission that her independence was more of a wish than a fact and, therefore, at least in part, a sham.

But if my father's illness deserves to be viewed in context, so does my mother's. Back then a lot of women were said to suffer from "nerves," a term used to describe a grab bag of female maladies that their male doctors neither understood nor, I suspect, cared to understand. I now recognize that my mother's nerves were often full-blown panic attacks. She would never be professionally diagnosed with obsessive-compulsive disorder, but as I wrote in my memoir, *Elsewhere*, all the signs were there. And she came by her condition rightly. As I said above, it was my grandmother who greeted me at the door each day when I came home from school. Indeed, it was she who walked me there each morning when I was in kindergarten and then home again when school got out, until I was old enough to make that four-block journey on my own. As a boy, nothing about this arrangement struck me as unusual. My mother worked and could not take me, and for the same reason neither could my grandfather. My grandmother did not work outside the home and therefore was available. That she would be available, every day, without fail, I took as perfectly normal. Nor did I give a single thought to the fact that outside the family she had no friends, not a single one. She would visit my aunt Phyllis, my mother's younger sister, who lived with her family a block and a half away, and on Sundays and holy days she attended Mass at Sacred Heart Church half a dozen blocks away. This was the length and breadth of my grandmother's world. Nor did she seem to want more. She never expressed the slightest desire to have any job other than that of housewife, never wished that she might meet a friend for lunch, never wanted to go away somewhere for a week or two in the summer, never even went with the rest of the family to the lake. There'd been a time, it was whispered, when she'd been terribly anxious, but that rough patch, I was given to understand, was long ago.

Over time, I began to suspect there was more to the story, but how much more I didn't learn until just a few years ago. It was Phyllis, my aunt, who finally confided the truth shortly before her own death. My grandmother hadn't just gone through a bad patch. Far from it. Rather, she'd battled crippling anxiety throughout her life. When my grandfather enlisted in the Second World War and was sent to the South Pacific, she became so paralyzed with ambient terror that she was barely able to leave the house. Convinced that she would become lost, she refused to go more than two or three blocks in any direction, and then always in a straight line. If she turned around and couldn't see the house she lived in, how would she find her way home? By this time my mother was in Georgia where my father was stationed, which left my aunt, then no more than twelve or thirteen, to take charge of anything that required a journey of more than a couple blocks. The good news was that this didn't happen often, and Phyllis was extraordinarily competent for her age. One night, though, they got a call from my mother, who announced that she and my father had decided to get married before he shipped overseas. In order for this to happen, they would need both her own and my father's birth certificates. His was at his parents' home in nearby Johnstown. What my mother wanted was for Phyllis and my grandmother to go there, explain the situation, obtain my father's birth certificate and mail both documents to Georgia.

Even now it's not clear to me whether my mother knew what she was asking. Johnstown was only three miles away. Did she know that she might as well have asked her mother to travel to the moon? Had her condition worsened since my grandfather left, or was her constant helpless agitation one of the reasons my mother decided to follow my father to Georgia? Nor do I know if my mother's own anxieties had begun to manifest yet. By her own account she'd been a free spirit back then, and the fact that at eighteen she hopped on a train and headed south on her own suggests that she was confident to the point of brashness. What story did she tell herself that would've made it okay for her to leave her mentally unsound mother in the care of her twelve-year-old sister? For that matter, what story did my grandfather, who'd already served in the First World War, tell himself that allowed him to enlist in his midforties for the Second, leaving his sick wife in the care of his daughters?

My aunt didn't speculate on any of this, but seventy years later her harrowing journey to Johnstown with my grandmother was still fresh in her mind: how she'd had to call for a taxi to take them, how my grandmother sat silently in the back seat smoothing her dress down over her knees again and again, how Phyllis had to coax her out of the cab, how my father's parents had had a hard time processing their request (Why would they hand over my father's birth certificate to people they'd never met?) and how it was she—Phyllis—who'd had to do the convincing while my grandmother sat in rigid silence, unable to utter a syllable to help her. I was in my late sixties when I first heard this story, and it rolled over me like a wave, forcing me to reconsider much of my childhood. Was it possible that all those years ago, when my grandmother was taking care of me, I was also, without knowing it, taking care of her, reducing the number of hours she would be alone, even as caring for me provided her with a sense of purpose? I'd been, I now saw, a duty she could manage. Yes, by then she was in better shape than she'd been during the war. My grandfather had returned. In ill health from a serious bout of malaria, he was no longer the man he'd been, but when she woke in the morning he was there, and when he went off to work at the glove shop it would be just a few short hours until he would return for lunch. He got off work at five, but unlike the men he worked with, he never stopped for a beer on the way home. When he climbed the front porch steps at five-ten, my grandmother was always at the front window peering through the blinds, where she'd been stationed for the last twenty minutes, knowing his return was imminent but unable to tear herself away from the window until she actually saw him round the corner, proof that she had not been left alone again. Neither she nor my grandfather ever went anywhere in the evening. We ate promptly at five-thirty.

By six-thirty the dishes were washed, dried and put away, and she and he were ensconced in front of the television. She was safe. During all those years, her world would never expand. She could hear my mother's and my footsteps overhead, and her other daughter's family lived nearby. On Sunday there was Mass. Otherwise, she went nowhere, and no one outside the family ever visited. Troubles that found her at home she could deal with, but she was finished with the outside world. This was my mother's genetic inheritance, that gift that keeps on giving.

But even this sad context deserves a wider lens. When I think back on my childhood and adolescence in Gloversville, I realize that chronic, debilitating anxiety was epidemic, that through-out our town's lower-middle-class neighborhoods other women were also battling with "nerves," women who were prescribed medications that altered their personalities or caused their hands to shake, not just under sudden stress, like my mother's, but constantly; women who startled when they were unexpect-edly spoken to; who were expected to make every dollar stretch at the corner store, even the dollars that got handed over to the bookies at the glove shops and the corner bars. When the drugs didn't work, some of these women were given shock treatments, which didn't work, either, but made them very, very quiet. And their hands stopped shaking. What they were suffering from, among other things, was the fact that they were women, which meant they got shitty pay and had little or no agency in the liv-ing of their own lives.

Okay, sure, you're thinking, *but so what?* Obviously, no mar-riage exists in a vacuum. All this context—cultural, historical, economic, genetic—provides a richer, more detailed picture, but does it make the resulting narrative more truthful? Is the result clarity, or does the additional information just muddy the waters? Doesn't the accumulation of detail also fly in the face of Occam's razor, which demands that we not "multiply entities" and reminds us the simplest explanation for the known facts is probably the best and truest? With so much else to consider, don't we run the risk of drifting that much further from the narrative's bedrock facts, which were never in dispute? My father was a compulsive gambler. His addiction was the proximate cause of my parents' marriage going on the rocks. Why am I unsatisfied with these simple facts and the clear narrative that results from them? Isn't it possible that my desire to multiply entities says more about me than the subject I'm investigating? I acknowledge this possibility here, not just because it will have occurred to readers, but also because I'm not finished with context. There's more to say about religion. And we've yet to talk about America.

2

During one of our many bitter arguments over the Vietnam War in the late sixties, my mother informed me that her only true religion had always been America. She said this proudly, defiantly, and I think when she said it, she honestly believed it. Indeed, the only word I'd take issue with is *always*, because by all accounts, my mother grew up a good Catholic girl, a product of Catholic schools. Even late in life, many years after she stopped going to church, she would surprise me with proclamations about the Roman Catholic Church being the one true faith. Though by then we would both have classified ourselves as agnostics, she was strangely proud of how little of her catechism she'd forgotten. She could still explain the difference between transubstantiation and consubstantiation, could expound at length upon why the Virgin Birth didn't mean what most people thought it did, could effortlessly classify which sins

qualified as venial and which were mortal. She'd been the sort
of girl, I suspect, for whom counting angels on the head of a
pin had come naturally, and even now it troubled her that my
break with the church had been so complete. It was as if she
imagined the day I might want to return to the fold and find
that my transgressions had been too great, that I had shut a
door tightly that she'd left purposely cracked, just in case. All
of this dovetailed with the woman I remembered from when
I was growing up, a woman who never missed Sunday Mass,
even though attendance couldn't have been easy for her, the
only woman in the congregation who was separated from her
husband. Still, if she had any quarrel with the church back
then, she never let on. As a boy I imagined we—that is, my
grandparents, my mother and I—were all on the same page,
all devout Catholics.

So, yes, I was surprised to hear my mother say, even in
anger, that America was her one and only true religion. The
more I thought about it, though, there had been discord in that
house we shared with my grandparents. As conflicts go, it had
been muted, a kind of ambient hum that I wasn't always able
to hear and could therefore easily ignore. But it had definitely
been there. I just hadn't been attuned to it. As I said above,
Catholicism was essential to my grandmother's everyday survival. All her life she'd used the church to quiet her fears and
give further structure to an already circumscribed life. By
contrast, my grandfather appeared merely to go through the
motions of faith. He was an usher at Sunday Mass, received
communion regularly, and never found excuses, as many men
did, to stay home when Sunday rolled around. But not once
when I was growing up did he ever suggest to me that the
church was important to him, nor did he ever suggest it should
be important to me. I have no memory of his ever going to

confession and find it hard to picture him, a proud man who'd served in two world wars, entering that dark booth and telling our haughty, ignorant German priest anything. Indeed, with a wink and a nod, he quietly mocked (for my cousins and me) the liturgy my grandmother considered sacred. I never heard him hint he didn't believe in the existence of God, but if God did exist, he was clearly the last thing on my grandfather's mind. Since returning from the South Pacific, he'd segued from one illness to the next, malaria to emphysema, his damaged lungs filling up with cigarette smoke and leather dust, until he had to fight for every breath. Knowing that my grandmother lived Sunday Mass to Sunday Mass, holy day to holy day, and that the comforts of religion were essential to her well-being, he simply went along.

But surely my mother took note of her father's quiet fifth-column rebellion against my grandmother's religiosity, and also saw it as a choice he was offering. If so, her eventually taking his side would have been a foregone conclusion. Refusing to acknowledge their temperamental similarity, my mother spent much of her life attempting to illustrate the many ways she and her mother were not only different but incompatible. She was also, as I suggested earlier, more than a little misogynistic. She much preferred the company of men and was more likely to take their advice. Ironically, it may have been my father who planted the seeds for her later rebellion. If she'd once been a good Catholic girl, it was clear that he'd never been a good Catholic boy. "Don't tell me you actually believe that horseshit," he scoffed when he found out that I'd become an altar boy. Had he said something similar to her at some point? I don't know, but the scene is easy enough to conjure.

One thing was certain. If the man who returned from the war wasn't the same as the one who left, neither was my mother the same girl my father married in Georgia. By the time she and I headed west in 1967, I for the University of Arizona, my mother for what she hoped would be a new life, her previous faith was relegated to the same rearview mirror she was putting Gloversville in. She now believed, with religious fervor, that as an American she had not just the right but the obligation to envision a better life, to leave the shackles of the past behind, to invent a new self to live that dreamed-of life. This new orthodoxy was nothing less than a manifesto, and like so many articles of faith it was born of repudiation. She saw our escape from Gloversville, its small-mindedness and parochialism, as her long-delayed (yes, delayed by me) birthright. Nor was this new manifesto just about herself. From the time I was a boy, she'd insisted that I could be anything I wanted to be. That was what the war her father and husband had fought in was really about. That was the America they'd been defending. The way she saw it now, our leaving our home and our loved ones was the proof of her new religion's power, its truth. Indeed, her conviction had become so strong that she couldn't remember ever having believed otherwise.

My father, who'd been part of the Normandy invasion and returned home a genuine war hero, shared few of my mother's core beliefs about the country he'd been defending. The war hadn't physically wrecked him as it had my grandfather, but if you compare photographs of him before shipping overseas with others taken in the Hürtgen Forest in Germany, you see a young man—a boy, really—segue into middle age in a matter of months. While my mother was watching patriotic newsreels at the Glove Theatre, he was advancing hedgerow to hedgerow through France, far in advance of the Allied supply chain, German soldiers surrendering faster than they could be processed. Often as not, he told me, they were taken down the road and shot. There was little glory in the war he remembered, only competence, and he suffered few illusions about the mission he'd undertaken on America's behalf. It was at once absolutely necessary and utterly soul destroying. When at last it was over, the man who returned was not, as my mother told me, the one who left, but how could he be? He'd done the terrible job that was demanded of him, and now, the way he looked at it, he was owed.

So it's not surprising that he would before long grow weary of my mother's patriotic optimism. Since the end of the war, she'd steadfastly maintained, and not without reason, that once the men came home the doors of opportunity that had been closed to people like her and my father (largely Catholics of Irish, Italian, Polish descent) would swing wide open. Having done everything that was asked of them without complaint, they would now be welcomed into America's many gated communities. The only thing holding any American back, she believed, was a lack of education, and that was being addressed by progressive legislations like the GI Bill and low-interest, government-backed student loans. Many other GIs were lining up to take advantage. What was wrong with my father that he showed so little interest? That question had answers, of course. Nearly all the young men my mother knew had served during the war, but not all saw combat, and relatively few saw the kind of fighting my father experienced as part of the D-Day invasion, not to mention the many months of trauma-inducing combat that followed as they made their way to Berlin. Such prolonged, eviscerating combat left men like my father disinclined to explain themselves when they returned home, certainly not to gung-ho women like my mother. Oh, sure, it would have been easy enough to destroy her innocence with his experience, but to what end? Far better to put that experience behind him, to lock the door of memory and throw away the key. As a result my mother found herself married to a stranger who made clear, day after day, that she could zig or zag, whichever she chose, but no amount of zigging or zagging was going to change his trajectory one iota. What a rude awakening this must've been. What on earth, she must have asked herself, was happening here?

Before she could figure it out, I came along. How did my mother react when she found out she was pregnant? I wish I knew. With little to go on and no one to ask, it's impossible to say for certain, but my advent had to alter the equation. By then it would have come home to her that dropping out of school and following my father to Georgia had been the biggest mistake of her life. But with so much water under so many bridges it would have been difficult for her to reverse course and go back to school. She was older now and not a girl anymore but rather a woman and a married one at that. Still, until I arrived on the scene, shifting gears had been possible. Now it wasn't. How her heart must've sunk to realize how thoroughly she'd managed to trap herself. Unless, of course, I've got it all wrong. Maybe I was part of a desperate plan. Maybe she got pregnant on purpose, hoping that a child would help her reel my father back in. If so, it was a terrible miscalculation. And yet, not an out-of-character one. As I would learn in the coming decades, my mother was always willing to risk making things worse—sometimes much worse—to achieve clarity. Not knowing was what she couldn't bear. In any event, now she knew. And when her pregnancy didn't alter my father's behavior, she had to know that it was over, that the happy, postwar life she'd imagined had at last gone up in smoke. I can imagine the combination of despair and profound bafflement she must have felt. How could she have gotten it all so terribly wrong? Thwarted everywhere she turned, what choice did she have but to accept defeat, to hunker down in the house my grandfather bought so we'd have a place to live? Under her mother's religious, watchful eye. Reminding herself, day after day, that she had a good job, that the little boy she'd given birth to was healthy and happy. Yes, things could've been worse. But, oh, was ever a woman so completely hemmed in, so utterly exiled for the foreseeable future from both opportunity and the possibility of joy? The days, months and years all strung out before her, her youth slipping away.

I suspect that what sustained her between the time she got pregnant and 1967 when she and I headed west was that slowly, slowly, as she watched this noisy, spirited, rambunctious kid of hers grow, a new plan began to take shape. Having watched her own ship disappear over the horizon without her, at some point it occurred to her that she might one day board mine. Yes, that vessel was still on the drawing board, but so what? Time was her long suit. She would oversee its design and construction, make certain it was seaworthy, maybe even help to chart its course. If she could somehow manage that, I would get the education she'd unwisely forsworn. Maybe she'd missed her own chance, but she'd make damn sure I didn't miss mine. She would badger me relentlessly to be at the top of my class so that I would qualify for scholarships and student loans. She would make sure I didn't get distracted by sports or, later, by girls. It wasn't the sort of plan you'd settle on if you had other options, but she didn't have any, so she focused on making this one work, and somehow it did. When I finished my BA at the university and decided to go for my master's, she cheered wildly, and cheered again when I enrolled in a PhD program in American literature. And why not? With each additional degree, her faith in American opportunity was further vindicated. The American Dream she believed in was alive and well in me. Somehow, she'd managed to keep me from mutiny and in so doing won that long-ago argument with my father about America. No one, including me, need know that she was actually the skipper of the vessel we were sailing.

Nor, as Barbara, my long-suffering wife, can attest, would she ever completely surrender the helm. In my late twenties, when I was finishing up that PhD and I announced that I intended not to be a college professor after all but rather a writer, my mother made no secret of her shock and dismay. My decision was not only foolish but dangerous. I was placing my family in harm's way. (She wasn't entirely wrong. My suddenly taking off in a new direction, so late in the overall scheme of things, was impulsive in the extreme.) It wasn't, I think, that she objected to my becoming a writer. Nor did she believe that such a goal was unobtainable for someone like me. Hadn't she drilled into me from the time I was a child that I could be whatever I wanted to be? Wasn't that my birthright, just as it had been hers back when we fled upstate New York? No, what she identified in my abrupt swerve away from the course she and I had charted was that despite her best efforts my father was still lurking, like a bent gene, in my otherwise carefully curated character. What I was doing, as she saw it, was gambling. In my sudden, overwhelming hunger to write fiction she recognized a fever similar to the one that overtook my father after his return from the war. Like him, I was suddenly in the grip of something stronger than I was. I would bet it all and lose, because that's what gamblers did. And, for all I know, an even-more-frightening thought may have occurred to her: What if it wasn't something in my father's character that was now manifesting in slightly altered form, but rather something in her own? Hadn't she herself, in following my father to Georgia, acted impulsively, her reason and good sense suddenly subverted? Was my choosing a romantic career (and, yes, it's true, writing has always been seen as a romantic vocation) over the more pragmatic one I'd trained long and hard for just an echo of her own error in judgment? Had it been inevitable from the start that something like this would happen? If so, wouldn't that suggest that the American Dream, her new religion, was itself a mere fantasy, a fable that we tell our children? That we tell ourselves to stave off despair?

And then, seemingly out of nowhere, a compromise. Instead of digging in my heels, I agreed to do the sensible thing, to finish my academic dissertation, my doctoral degree, and go on the job market. I would become, for a time at least, the academic my mother (and, yes, my wife, as well) wanted me to be, and leave writing stories to my spare time. The urge to roll the dice might have prevailed if I'd been single, but I was a husband and father, so I dutifully raised the sails of the vessel we'd embarked in back in 1967, brought it at last into port and dropped anchor. Though my heart wasn't in it, I prepared for life as a university professor.

My first academic posting was at a branch campus of Penn State University. Barbara was then pregnant with our second daughter, so my father flew west to help me drive a crammed U-Haul truck back East. Barbara would follow as soon as I found us a place to live. The cross-country journey took several days, and it was the most time I'd spent with my father since the summers we worked road construction nearly a decade earlier. He'd aged, but his body was still hard and lean from a life of unremitting physical labor. "What's that?" he said, our first day on the road. He'd noticed the paunch I'd been working on for some time. "That's what you get when you sit in a library for ten years straight," I admitted. When we arrived in Pennsylvania, I drove directly to the pretty little campus so I could show my father where I'd be teaching. It was an early afternoon in August and the campus was empty. I turned off the ignition, and we just sat. I don't remember what I said in the silence, but it must've been optimistic, something my mother would have agreed with, because my father snorted. "You do know your name ends in a vowel, right?" When I asked him what that was supposed to mean, he was all too happy to elaborate. "It means they're only going to let you get so far." I knew better than to follow him down this particular rabbit hole, having done so many times in the past with little to show for it, but I couldn't help myself. "Who is *they*, exactly?" My father shook his head. "All that education," he sighed, "and you still don't know who they are?"

You see, unlike my mother, my father didn't believe things had changed much after the war. To him postwar America was a place where cops parked down the street from the bars where workingmen drank but not the cocktail lounges frequented by lawyers and doctors. If guys in suits did manage to get pulled over for drunk driving, their arrests somehow didn't make it into the local paper. They, my father explained, were the people who had guys like him—the men who fought their wars for them—by the balls. They had money and power, and they weren't shy about using it, either. And their names did not end in vowels. Okay, sure, he'd just driven across the country with his son, the newly minted Dr. Russo, and, yes, he was willing to concede that education had removed some significant barriers. My life would be easier than his had been. The cops wouldn't be waiting outside the bars where I drank, and the color of my skin was one full shade lighter than his own, which also helped. But he wanted me to understand that some doors would never open to me for the simple reason that America was still America. At the time, I thought we were arguing about class, but now I'm sure that was only part of it. My mother believed that the man she married—handsome, charming Jimmy Russo—was white, that the war had settled, once and for all, how Italian Americans should be viewed. Yes, there'd been a time when they, especially dark-skinned Italians, had been seen as "colored," but those days, she was certain, were gone. My father, having been called a guinea and a wop when he was a boy, was less sanguine on the subject. His family's road to assimilation had been far from smooth. Like my maternal grandfather, his father had also been a craftsman. Back in Italy he'd made fine men's shoes. In America, where men didn't buy custom-made shoes, at least not in upstate New York, he'd become a lowly shoe-repair man and was treated accordingly. And there was also something else, something, well, darker. Many of the Italian Americans my father knew were far from color-blind themselves. Lighter-skinned, "bean eating" northerners were deeply prejudiced against "garlicky," olive-skinned southerners. "What's the matter?" I remember him kidding another Italian American man who'd married a southerner. "You couldn't find a white girl?" It was said in jest, of course, but for my father skin color was no joking matter. By late August, after working for months under a blazing sun, he could pass for Black himself until he took his shirt off. Even if my mother was right and the war had made him white, that didn't mean his new status couldn't be taken away by subsequent events. And it certainly didn't mean that any son of his would be living in a class- and race-blind country.

My mother and father both died believing they were right about America.

3

So, who was right? It occurs to me that I have been pondering America—my grandparents', my parents' and mine—for decades, attempting to reconcile, at least for my own edification, our various and disparate American experiences. In the end my novels, stories and essays may be little more than a record of this internal conversation.

In many respects I'm a poster boy for the American Dream my mother believed in until the day she died. I'm a product of public schools and the same low-interest, government-backed student loans my mother saw as our ticket out of Gloversville and into a new, better life out West. I am, on both sides of my family, of immigrant stock—Italian, Irish, French, German. Moreover, despite a lack of material resources when I was young and my relatively undistinguished academic pedigree, not many doors have been closed to me, and the few that were I had little desire to walk through anyway. The America my mother prepared me for was closer to the America of my experience than the one my father feared might have it in for me. It could also be argued that optimism has a way of paying dividends that pessimism rarely does. In America, pessimists are more likely to be right, optimists more likely to succeed.

The thing my father got most right, though, was that America didn't fundamentally change after the war. The hero's welcome he got when he returned from overseas was different from the welcome Black GIs got, especially those returning to the South. Nor was it just the South. In Gloversville, when I was growing up, petitions circulated when Black families tried to buy homes on our modest street, and the little starter home in a new development on the outskirts of town that my mother had her eye on would've been redlined. The low-interest, government-backed loans I took advantage of were far less available to dark-skinned people. Maybe America didn't have it in for me, but there were those it did systemically disadvantage, and it's the legacy of that disadvantage—our refusal to admit to it or discuss the reparations such injustice demands—that fuels our ongoing culture wars. Writing about these conflicts in *The New York Times,* columnist Tom Friedman argues that what Trump supporters are most attracted to is his willingness to demonize the educated elites who look down on them, who consider them to be, in Hillary Clinton's famous phrase, a "basket of deplorables." Trumpers, Friedman explains, will cheerfully accept further economic depredations, provided the educated liberal elites they despise (yes, like me) are taken down a peg or two. Why, they want to know, is the so-called meritocracy not content to congratulate its winners? Why must those who have defined *merit* to suit themselves also denigrate those who don't measure up? The way they see it, they've been not just left behind but humiliated, and my father, having himself been humiliated, would've understood that. Having been part of the Normandy invasion, he wouldn't have fallen for a phony grifter like Cadet Bone Spur, but he would've understood his supporters because their experience of life was not so terribly different from his own. He also would've seen Democrats as largely taking the white working class for granted and thus making Republicans of them. Like many Trump supporters, my father believed he was playing against a stacked deck.

The only time in her life my mother ever voted Republican was for Ronald Reagan in 1980. She despised everything about the sixties—hippies, protests, rock and roll, peace marches, weed—and she saw Reagan as a necessary corrective. Though she had despised Nixon, she believed in America's military might, supported the war in Vietnam and, like both Reagan and Trump, was all in on law and order. But unlike my father, she wouldn't have understood Trump voters at all. To her way of thinking, their long list of grievances would've all come down to this: they should've done better in school. If they'd gotten that college degree, they would've ended up on the right side of the class divide instead of the wrong one. They had nobody but themselves to blame. Anyone who desired proof could just have a look at me, her son, who started out on the wrong side of the economic tracks in a small, depressed Rust Belt town. In her telling, instead of feeling ill used, I simply worked hard and took advantage of what America had to offer. Her advice to Trump supporters would've been to quit their bellyaching. We wear the chains we forge in life. End of story. The fact that other chains existed (genetic, racial, historical) that were forged before we were born either didn't enter her thinking at all or were dismissed as excuses for failure.

Few things in my mother's life, especially as she got older, hurt her more deeply than my refusal, as she saw it, to take her side in matters large and small. She always considered such demurrals on my part betrayals, and probably some of them were. Proud of my accomplishments and quick to run them up her personal flagpole, she was ever my ferocious defender, even when I was clearly in the wrong. Why, she often wondered out loud, couldn't I return the favor every now and then? Didn't I remember how nice it had been back when we were of one mind, when we saw the world the same way? When we steered toward a common, agreed-upon future? How was this new reality, this constant ideological friction, an improvement over our old harmony? I fear that at some point I became like my father, disinclined to explain things, and for that I'm probably to blame. Maybe there was a way to help her understand that, to me, her late-in-life American Dream narratives were a lot like her earlier explanation for the breakup of her marriage to my father: changed by the war, he'd come home sick, a compulsive gambler; to save both herself and me, she had no choice but to banish him from our lives. The story was clear, simple, coherent and not directly contradicted by any of the known facts.

The same can be said of the story she liked to tell of my university triumphs, as well as my later successes as a teacher and writer. Not surprisingly, it lasers in on hard work and ingenuity, those most central of American virtues. It's a familiar narrative that derives from Horatio Alger bootstrap mythology, and it largely ignores other powerful forces (that is, history and science) that also shape human destiny, forces that would have complicated a story she preferred to keep simple and straightforward. She simply couldn't wrap her head around my perverse refusal to accept her flattering account of my accomplishments. How, otherwise, could she share in them? What prevented me from conceding the justice of her conviction that hard work, together with American opportunity, yielded success, just as she'd always maintained?

Well, for starters, before I could even begin to measure the labors involved in earning a doctoral degree and later becoming a writer, I immediately got tripped up by the word *work*, which took me back to those summers I spent doing construction with my father. If you haven't put in an eleven-hour day in ninety-degree heat as a grader on a road crew, I'd argue that your education into the world of work is incomplete. Allow me to explain. The major roads we all drive on are concrete, which is poured into the space between parallel, heavy metal forms that later, after the concrete has set, are pulled away and reused. Before these forms can be laid out, though, the ground has to be absolutely level, and to this end wooden stakes are driven into the earth and strings attached. A "grader" works with a shovel that is notched, so that when the blade is stood on end the notch lines up with the string. Where the ground is too high, dirt has to be scraped away; where it's too low, it must be added and tamped down. It's a job that simply can't be done standing up straight. The angle that you bend at the waist— think seven minutes to twelve on a clock—doesn't seem severe until you try to maintain that posture hour after hour. Trying to straighten up at the end of the day is akin to a religious experience, and finally achieving that upright stance, even for a twenty-year-old, as I was back then, is nearly orgasmic. Imagine doing that every day for twenty or thirty years, like some of the guys I worked with. If you can't, congratulations, but I can, and it's the reason that even after three decades as a—yes— hardworking writer, when people talk to me about how hard they work at their demanding white-collar jobs, I find myself right back on that road crew, and my still-vivid memories of that backbreaking job never fail to remind me that one of the reasons I became first a professor and then a novelist was that I didn't want to do that job or any other like it for the rest of my life. So pause and imagine for a moment what it must feel like to do that kind of work over a lifetime and then be looked down on by somebody who writes fucking code. The problem with my mother's flattering narrative about how hard I worked to achieve success is that I've actually done hard work and I know the difference.

Please understand. I don't mean to be dismissive here. My mother's pride in my accomplishments was born of love, but in the end love may not be the best lens through which to view reality. It led her, for example, to confuse what she saw as my disadvantages in life with what I would belatedly come to recognize as my greatest advantages. It's true, of course, that the upstate mill town where I grew up offered few economic opportunities, and my mother's conviction that remaining there would have been tantamount to economic suicide wasn't far off the mark. But it's also true that my childhood there was not unhappy. Despite my parents' separation and our family's being relatively poor, I was surrounded, thanks to my mother, my grandparents and my aunt Phyllis and her family, by love. When I decided to become a writer, I mastered the craft elements of storytelling—character development, conflict, dialogue, setting—pretty quickly, but then my progress suddenly and unexpectedly ground to a halt. Though I didn't know it at the time, the biggest obstacle between me and success as a writer had exactly nothing to do with the tools of my trade but rather a breathtaking lack of self-knowledge. A decade after leaving my hometown, I was still seeing it through my mother's eyes as a place to flee. After all, that's what we'd done. It must've been necessary, or we wouldn't have done it, right? Though my mother had never instructed me to be ashamed of where I was from, that was the message I got, loud and clear. Given the many sacrifices she'd made on my behalf, I went along, seeing things her way or at least pretending to. Why? Well, probably because at the time it seemed like her having one loyal ally in the world, even if it was a twelve-year-old, was all that was holding her together.

There are few hard-and-fast rules about becoming a writer, or any kind of artist, for that matter, but one thing I can state with absolute certainty is that no matter how gifted you are, or how hardworking, you're never going to be any good until you know who and what you love, because until then you won't know who you are. It took me far too long to understand what now couldn't be more obvious—that I was born in exactly the right place at exactly the right time. Like Faulkner, I'd been gifted the perfect lens through which to view America. Perhaps even more important, I'd been given the perfect parents and extended family, the perfect neighborhood and hometown, through which to examine my country's myriad brutal contradictions. My childhood had not been a disadvantage at all. It would become my greatest strength if I only let it.

But know this. If loyalty to my mother resulted in a kind of blindness and confusion that were difficult for me, even as an adult, to surmount, her unflagging loyalty to me came at an even-larger price. For as long as she could convince herself that she and I saw things the same way, I think she believed that her sacrifices had paid off. After a rocky start, she'd finally gotten it right. We'd made a clean getaway from Gloversville, and now at last the breeze was at our backs. When I published my first novel and her dire predictions about my changing course so abruptly didn't come to pass, she concluded that she'd dodged a final bullet. We would all be fine. Still, that first book had to unnerve her. The fictional town of the title—Mohawk—was clearly modeled on Gloversville, and several of its characters would have been instantly recognizable to her. It was only one book, though. I would write others. But with each new novel a reality she didn't want to acknowledge was becoming more and more evident. Our getaway had been anything but clean for either of us. After a second marriage didn't work out and my mother's anxieties reappeared with a vengeance, she'd had no choice but to return to Gloversville, to the house we shared with my grandparents, where at least she would be safe. I myself would never live in my hometown again, but each new book revealed that, in a sense, I'd never really left. "Do you think you'll ever write about people with clean fingernails?" she once asked me wistfully, and there was neither anger nor resentment in the observation, just defeat. Each book was further evidence that we no longer saw things the same way and never would again. For that to happen she'd have to be thirty-five again and I twelve. Hers is a very American story, I think. Trapped in an unjust world, you light out for the western territories, like Huck Finn. Or, like Gatsby, you attempt to leave the past behind by creating a new and better self to pursue the green light of happiness, so close you can almost touch it, never suspecting it's an optical illusion.

My father fared better, perhaps because, after Normandy, he had fewer illusions about either America or himself. He could be more honest with the man he confronted in the mirror each morning. After spending a decade or more in the poker rooms above the pool hall, he managed, with the help of a woman who could not have been more unlike my mother, to find his way out of them. Though he never expressed it to me, I know he felt guilty that after he was banished from our lives, he let me go without a fight, never really trying to be part of my young life. And I suspect he understood that when I became a father myself my game plan was simple: to never not be there when my children needed me. If that was a repudiation, he didn't seem to resent or dwell on it. My novels are full of stuff that would've made him cringe, but he was spared all that by dying in his late sixties before the first one came out. My mother was in her mideighties when she was diagnosed with congestive heart failure and told she had only another year or two to live. At the time she was living in an apartment house just a few blocks from where my wife and I lived. ("Oh, I live independently," she liked to tell people.) She had one friend, her next-door neighbor, and she seldom left her apartment except to join us for dinner or when I took her grocery shopping. My father, right to the end, lurched through the world from barstool to barstool, still getting pulled over by cops who sat in the shadows outside bars where guys like him drank, though by then they all knew him by name, and most let him off with a warning and a promise to go straight home, a promise that was, they both knew, nonbinding. If he had any late-in-life grievances, he left them unvoiced. He and America had by then come to an accommodation. Neither would attempt to change the other. At his memorial service the crowd spilled out of the largest of the funeral home's viewing rooms and into the other two. So very little in life is even remotely fair.

As I write this, America is coming apart at the seams, thanks to a raging pandemic, deepening income inequality, systemic racial injustice, shockingly routine gun violence, a sociopathic president who refuses to concede defeat in a fair election and a Republican Party that refuses, as it has all along, to constrain him because it's in their short-term interest not to. In the months leading up to the election many of my friends talked about leaving the country if he won a second term. Not me. The idea of living in a more just, more decent country is appealing, I admit, but I know I'm not going anywhere. I've learned that leaving your home is tricky. If I left my country now, I'd just be repeating myself, having already physically left a place that refused to leave me. My grandfather wouldn't leave. And despite not being able to agree on what America really meant, neither would either of my parents. Maybe it comes down to this: In the end, what do we do with love? At this point I feel the need to express straightforwardly that which I would hope need not be said at all. I love my country, and though they are all gone now, I love the people in this essay—my mother and father, my maternal grandparents—to the very bottom of my heart. In life, they were as full of flaws and contradictions as the country they too loved. My father was deeply prejudiced against Black people, but his best friend was Black. My mother was both

misogynistic and homophobic, but I'm absolutely certain that
if one of her granddaughters had turned out to be a lesbian,
she would've simply pivoted away from ideology and loved her
fiercely anyway. Like her mother before her, mine lived much
of her life in terror, yet at the same time both these women were
capable of the kind of courage to which I can only aspire. My
grandfather, gasping for breath and, in his later years, tethered
to an oxygen tank, continued to sneak out into the backyard
for a smoke whenever my grandmother wasn't looking. We get
to love such people. Face it. We are, most of us, a mess. We get
to love our country, too, and for the same reason. America has
never not been a mess.

Still, all that admitted to, how many accommodations does
love demand? How much loyalty? As Tom Friedman argues,
we do well to listen carefully to our political adversaries, but
surely there are things decent people should not be required
to listen to. Humiliation may not be in anyone's interest, and
categorizing certain of our fellow citizens as "deplorable" is not
only unkind but unwise, but that doesn't mean that deplorable
behavior must be tolerated. Last year my Latino brother-in-law
and his wife were invited to a holiday party composed of family
and friends. The women were all in the kitchen, the men having gathered in the living room. There was probably a sporting
event on, but for whatever reason, the other guys didn't immediately see my brother-in-law join them, so he got to hear them
discuss how much better off the country would be if it could be
rid of all Black people and Mexicans. Marilynne Robinson has
recently reminded us that America is more than an idea; it's
also a family. Tell that to my brother-in-law. Tell that to George
Floyd's family.

Nations, like individuals, crave the comfort of simple, stream-
lined narratives, even when those don't bear close scrutiny. We

like to tell our children that American wealth derives from American hard work and ingenuity, a marriage of great natural resources and exceptional national character. Why muddy the waters by informing them that many of those resources were stolen from the indigenous peoples, that much of our communal and personal wealth derives from the free labor of African slaves, that the authors of the Declaration of Independence, who declared that all men were created equal, really meant by *men* a small subset of the population: white, male landowners. If the narrative we tell our kids about America is like the one my mother told me about her breakup with my father, what happens when they're older and come to view what we told them through a wider lens and take into account the context we hoped they wouldn't notice? When they ask us why we oversimplified the story, will our only defense be to remind them how happy they were when they were kids and we were all on the same page and saw the same things the same way? Will we say to them, *Remember how we used to love each other? Back when we didn't fight?*

More than anything, what I think we're all wondering is whether what we're living through right now is a breakup story. We keep hearing that there are two Americas: one rich and one poor, one Black and one white, one red and one blue, one educated and one not. If those Americas are going through a divorce, how will our grandchildren tell that story? Will they conclude that it was tragic and preventable? Or will they remember us as ill-matched from the start and conclude that it was only a matter of time before our differences became irreconcilable? One thing seems certain: the simpler and more straightforward their narrative is, the more likely it is to be untrue.

What We Really Want
from Stories

When it became clear that my parents were going to split up, my maternal grandfather bought a modest, two-family house in our upstate New York mill town so that my mother and I would have a place to live. He and my grandmother occupied the downstairs flat, my mother and I the identical upstairs one. She paid rent, but even as a kid I knew we were being subsidized, that there was no way my mother could afford our flat at its market value. Nor was this our only subsidy. Because my mother worked at GE in Schenectady, an hour away, she was gone before I awoke most mornings, and she didn't return until after I'd eaten an early dinner with my grandparents. It was my grandmother who walked me to school, a mere four blocks away, until I was old enough to undertake that journey on my own, and it was she who greeted me when I returned midafternoon. To pass the time, she taught me her favorite card games—gin rummy and pitch—and we played these by the hour on the living room sofa, its center cushion serving as a table. We would quit between four-thirty and five, after which she would station herself at the front window to await my grandfather's return from the glove shop where he worked, which he always did promptly. Not once in the eighteen years I lived with them did my grandfather stop for a beer with the guys. I understood that he and, especially, my grandmother were looking after me in my mother's absence, allowing her to have what she called a "real job," unlike the other neighborhood mothers, who either stayed home or worked in the skin mills like their husbands.

When you're a kid, normal is what you experience every day, and that includes people, especially the ones you love. It didn't strike me as particularly odd that my grandmother should be my primary caregiver, at least on weekdays, because our circumstance (my parents' separation) was unusual. *Of course*, my grandmother would fill the void that separation created. Nor did I wonder why she had no friends in the neighborhood, why no one ever dropped by for a visit except my aunt Phyllis, my mother's younger (by six years) sister and her family, who lived around the corner. That my grandfather had no friends either was, to my mind, explained by the fact he'd returned from the Pacific with malaria, from which he'd never fully recovered. Except when he was at work, my grandparents' lives were lived in that house. They never went out to dinner or to the lake in the summer with the rest of the family. They ventured out only on Sundays and holy days to attend Mass at the church where my grandfather served as an usher. Though there was a corner store at the end of the street, our groceries were ordered over the phone and delivered.

NOW, IN MY SEVENTIES, I marvel at how seldom I questioned the narrative of the first eighteen years of my life. Because something, obviously, wasn't right. *My* normal wasn't normal at all. Only after my mother and I moved to Arizona and I enrolled in the university there, returning home in the summers to work road construction with my father, did I begin to glimpse how unusual things had been and continued to be in my grandparents' house. By then my grandfather had been diagnosed with the emphysema that would eventually kill him, and the perimeter of their lives had shrunk even further. With my mother and me gone, they rented the upstairs flat we'd occupied, so there was no reason for them to leave their downstairs one. By then my grandfather was often too ill to attend Sunday Mass, so it fell to my aunt to make sure my grandmother got to church. I took up residence in their spare bedroom those summers, doing what I could on weekends around the house—painting, taking off the storm windows, mowing the lawn—things my grandfather had taken great pride in doing until he became tethered to the oxygen tank that now sat behind his armchair. Enlightenment came in dribs and drabs. One day, on the way home from work, my father casually asked me if I'd twigged to the fact that my mother was crazy, the answer to which was both yes and no. I knew—had always known—that she suffered from crippling anxiety, that it was only her meds that allowed her to live a somewhat-normal life, but I had no idea that her illness had a name (obsessive-compulsive disorder) and could be treated if diagnosed (she never was). But the real revelation was about my grandmother, and that one came only after both she and my mother died. According to my aunt, she too had suffered from debilitating anxiety her entire life. So acute was her terror that as a young woman she'd been unable to venture more than a few blocks from the rented apartment where she, my grandfather and their daughters lived, and then always in a straight line, convinced that if she lost sight of the building, she'd never find her way home. Only then, as a grown man with a family of my own, did it dawn on me that maybe, those afternoons when

I came home from school to find her nervously waiting for me with a deck of cards in her hand, I was taking care of her as much as she was taking care of me, that she was still afraid to leave the house. Which meant that the entire narrative of my childhood and adolescence was in play.

WHAT IS IT that we search for in stories? Answers? Explanations? Understanding? Maybe, but in my experience, answers provide only temporary gratification and reassurance for the simple reason that they almost always beget other questions and often result in uncomfortable ambiguities we've little choice but to accept. When my aunt revealed that as a young wife and mother, my grandmother had been paralyzed by incapacitating anxieties, yes, it explained some things that had been nagging at me since I was a kid. *Okay, good,* I told myself, *I wasn't imagining that.* But trailing in the wake of my new understanding and appreciation of my grandmother's behavior and the suffering that occasioned it was a profound mystery. Given her condition, why in the world had my grandfather enlisted in World War II? He was far too old to be drafted. I'd always believed it was because it was the patriotic thing to do, and my grandfather had never been one to shirk a moral duty, even if it meant going to the other side of the world and risking his life in the defense of freedom, our way of life and, yes, his family. Didn't that narrative square perfectly with everything I knew about the man? Maybe, but it didn't align terribly well with what I'd just learned. *He'd actually left his mentally ill wife in the care of his young daughters?* Panicked, I immediately went in search of justifications. *Okay,* I thought, *I know now that what Mother and Grandmother suffered from is classified as mental illness, but he didn't.* He would have thought of it, as most people (or at least most men) did back then, as a simple case of nerves. And if that's all it was, then my mother, who was eighteen when my grandfather shipped overseas, was surely old enough to assume that responsibility. Nor could he have known that he'd no sooner be out the door than my mother, who may have told herself the same thing (that her mother was just nervous), would decide to head south and join my father where he was stationed in Georgia, leaving my grandmother in the care of Mother's twelve-year-old sister. Reluctantly, I had to wonder if my grandfather, a smart, gifted man who'd never had the opportunity to showcase those gifts, had seen the war as an opportunity to shed, at least temporarily, the iron shackles of his life in our small mill town. When he returned home after the war, a man only barely recognizable as the one who left, did he see his being once again securely tethered to the glove shop, to his marriage and family, to the Catholic church and, in the end, to an oxygen tank, to be just retribution for having used the war as an excuse to flee the life he'd long been trapped in? The answer to this question resides right where it belongs, in his heart, in that private place we all have and deserve to have, where our motives, seldom clear, often lurk in the shadows. Such mystery, I suspect, is what we're really looking for in stories. If my grandfather's motives were ambiguous, his story is that much more moving, that much more heartbreaking. And I love him more, not less.

Ghosts

Route 29

The whole idea of a midsummer book tour is new to me, and it feels very, very strange. Instead of hopping on planes bound for big cities, where readers and media tend to concentrate, I'm driving (Barbara, my wife, is actually at the wheel) to where those same people gather to escape the summer heat: places like Cape Cod and the Berkshires and coastal Connecticut. And, of course, Saratoga Springs, the real upstate New York city that inspired my fictional Schuyler Springs, the lucky town of my *Fool* novels. In the last of these, the book I'm currently promoting, Schuyler has just devoured North Bath, its unlucky neighbor. Because Saratoga is close to Gloversville, the mill town where I grew up, there are lots of people at the event who I have some sort of personal connection to. We were once neighbors or classmates, or they knew members of my family, my maternal grandparents, my mother, my father—all long dead now, though they are my ghostly companions whenever I visit upstate New York. Every third person in the signing line seems to have a story to share, which makes for a long evening. I'm due back in Portland for an event at my daughter's bookstore the following day, but rather than head directly there, my wife and I drive to Gloversville instead. I haven't seen my cousin Greg and his wife, Carole, in quite a while, and they weren't able to attend the Saratoga event.

Measured in miles Gloversville isn't far, but this morning I'm not measuring in miles. Rather, I'm awash in metaphor (a writerly occupational hazard) and memory (a natural consequence of getting old). But even as a young man I understood that the thirty-mile stretch of narrow, two-lane blacktop between Saratoga and my hometown was a journey from relative affluence to scarcity, from good fortune to ill. No sooner do you leave Saratoga's city limits on Route 29 than everything begins to look scruffier. That was true fifty years ago, and it's even truer now. Most of the welcoming roadhouses my father and I used to stop at on our way home from the horse track back in the 1970s have survived but only just. Their shabby façades bring to mind James McMurtry's 2005 song, "We Can't Make It Here," where "The bar's still open but, man, it's slow / The tip jar's light and the register's low / The bartender don't have much to say / The regular crowd gets thinner each day." What, I wonder, would my father make of these gone-to-seed establishments? He never believed, as my mother did, that the Second World War would fundamentally change America, that its various private clubs and institutions would throw open their doors and put out the welcome mat for returning veterans and their families. Oh, sure, thanks to the GI Bill and other postwar legislation, I might have a few more opportunities than he'd had, but I don't think he foresaw that my life would be radically different from his own.

Still, if he didn't expect things to be much better, I don't think he imagined them getting much worse, either. It wouldn't have occurred to him that our old Route 29 watering holes would ever fall on hard times. After all, how could you fail to make money selling cheap, cold beer to thirsty workingmen? Not having a crystal ball, there was no way for him to foresee that in the not-that-distant future many of the jobs he and his friends did would be lost to globalization or automation. He believed, as most of us do, that tomorrow would be pretty much like today. Okay, maybe the next generation of guys like him wouldn't be able to buy a house in Saratoga, but surely they'd be able to visit now and then, to rub shoulders on a warm summer afternoon with the moneyed, well-dressed folks who drove up from the city for the track or to hear a concert at Performing Arts. It didn't particularly bother him that they got to stay there and he got to go home because, to his way of thinking, home wasn't so bad, and Route 29 got you there gradually, one welcoming roadhouse at a time. Why would he imagine that the day would come when a lot of guys like him simply couldn't make it here anymore?

Channeling

Because it happens every single time I visit Gloversville, I'm not surprised to feel the tightness in my chest, the old familiar dread, as Barbara and I near our destination. I try not to see my hometown through my mother's eyes, but it's hard not to. God, how she hated the place, and why not? She spent most of the nearly two decades that we lived above my grandparents in their two-family house on Helwig Street dreaming of escape. Legally separated but still married to my father, she felt her parents' unblinking, judgmental eye on her day and night. On those rare occasions when she went out on dates, always with men she knew from GE in Schenectady where she worked, she was careful to go somewhere that she wouldn't be spotted by people from Gloversville who would report back that she, a married woman, had been seen in public with a man who was not her husband. It would've been easy enough to cut and run if she'd been willing to abandon me, but she wasn't. Instead, she kicked the can down the road, patiently planning her eventual escape to coincide with my going off to college, hoping—praying, really—that there would be enough of her youth left for her to make up for lost time. GE had a shop of some sort in Phoenix, so maybe there. She'd heard that life would be both cheaper and easier in Arizona, and even if it wasn't, at least she'd be free. With Gloversville in her rearview mirror, she'd have a clean slate. She could start over.

But, of course, wherever you go, there you are. My mother had hoped that the debilitating panic attacks she suffered from in Gloversville would abate, that she wouldn't require Valium to keep her hands from shaking, but if anything, her condition worsened. Back home, though she rarely needed to, she could float a small loan from my grandparents to tide her over until payday. No longer. Worse, the social life she'd been denied, the freedom she craved for so long, proved elusive. There were a few single guys in the apartment house where she rented a one-bedroom, but most of the men she came in contact with were married. She'd hoped to get hired at GE, but the Phoenix shop turned out to be little more than a warehouse, and in any case there were no openings and none were anticipated. Eventually, she did meet and fall in love with a charming but feckless man who didn't love her back. Then, trying a different tack, met and married a man who *did* love her but offered little in the way of charm or style, and after so many years of deprivation she required both. When their marriage failed, she had little choice but to return home, what remained of her youth spent, to the same house on Helwig Street that her whole family had warned her not to leave in the first place. There, she found herself even more securely tethered to the town she loathed. Before, she'd had a good job in Schenectady, whereas now, having burned her GE bridges, she had little choice but to take a job as a bookkeeper at a local accounting firm, where she made barely enough to cover her living expenses. Nobody said I told you so, but then nobody had to. She'd gambled and lost. There was nothing to do but admit defeat and accept that dreams, no matter how vivid or necessary, were just that—dreams. At least, she told herself, she'd gotten me out. I was doing well at the University of Arizona. I would become the English professor she wanted me to be and enter a safe, secure life on my own terms, Gloversville a distant memory.

She toughed it out there on Helwig Street for as long as she could, but eventually her life began to spiral. By then I'd finished my graduate work and gotten married, and my wife and I had two daughters. When I got the call from my aunt describing my mother's mental state, Barbara and I had little choice but to rescue her. From then on, for the rest of her life, my mother lived wherever we did. It wasn't the life she dreamed of, of course. She wanted a life of her own, not one tethered to ours. Despite working hard her whole life, her meager social security benefit wasn't sufficient to make ends meet, but by then I'd become a writer and published a couple novels, and it was easy enough to bridge the financial gap. Over time she came to the painful realization, as my father would have if he'd lived long enough, that she couldn't make it here anymore, at least not on her own. But she loved watching her granddaughters grow up, and at least she was no longer in Gloversville. In her eighties, when she became ill and knew the end was near, our hometown was still on her mind, and it wasn't where she wanted to end up, even in death. By then, if she believed in God at all, it was in one who might play just this kind of cruel trick on her, and she was determined to thwart his divine will, if possible. Her end-of-life wishes were clear and simple. She wanted to be cremated, her ashes scattered anywhere but Gloversville. I gave her my word that I would make this happen.

All of which accounts for the creeping dread I feel as my wife and I make our way along Route 29. Weirdly, my penchant for channeling my mother's desperation whenever I return home has gotten worse since her death, to the point that it will contaminate my own thinking, causing me to wonder if my having facilitated her final escape, Gloversville might claim me instead, an even-crueler version of the trick my mother feared God would play on her. It doesn't help that, despite being an altar boy all the way through high school, my own idea of God, when I can bring myself to believe in him at all, isn't so different from hers. (One of my favorite jokes: *You want to make God laugh? Tell him your plans.*) I know, of course, that to be channeling my mother's suffering at this late date is completely batshit. All I can say is try living the first eighteen years of your life with a parent who cycles from one enervating panic attack to the next, and see if you yourself are always rational.

Anyway, by the time we get to the end of Route 29, I've managed to calm down. I remind myself that my mother's Gloversville is not my own and never has been, that my childhood and adolescence there were just fine. I had loving grandparents and cousins around the corner and lots of friends. I did well in school and played sports and dated pretty girls. I'm also aware of the irony of my circumstance: I'm an author on book tour. For three decades my fiction has centered on place and class, on people who have a hard time making it here. For a writer like me, it's hard to imagine a better place to be from than poor, snakebit Gloversville. Had I been "luckier" and grown up in

Saratoga, a child of privilege, would I even be a writer today? I have my doubts. Art—all art—thrives on conflict, the more tangled and impossible to unravel the better. It took a while, but I've come to recognize my profound debt to the town my mother was so determined to spare me. Some years ago, in an attempt to demonstrate that gratitude, I became a visible public face and voice of a fundraising effort to restore the beautiful old Carnegie library that was a lifeline when I was a boy. During that surprisingly successful campaign, it seemed to me that maybe, just maybe, my unlucky hometown had finally turned a corner. Along Main Street there were small signs of renewal, tiny green shoots of economic life sprouting—a new co-op on Main Street, the refurbished Glove Theatre. And so, arriving on the outskirts of town, I take a deep breath and vow to see the place through my father's eyes, not my mother's. After all, by the time *he* got to the end of Route 29, he wasn't unhappy to be home. If things were shabby and opportunity scarce, so what? His life was here. It wasn't Saratoga, but it was his home, and I tell myself that it's mine, too.

At any rate, here we are. I've just about convinced myself that everything will be fine when we make the turn off Kingsboro Avenue and onto Fifth and enter my old neighborhood. That's when the gut punch comes.

Ladders

If Gloversville was the perfect place for me to grow up in order for me to become the writer I am today, then Helwig Street, where my grandparents' house was located, together with adjacent Sixth Avenue, where my aunt and uncle and cousins lived, was the perfect neighborhood. Summers, boys like my cousins and me mowed our elderly neighbors' lawns, raked their leaves in the fall and shoveled their sidewalks in the winter. We were paid in crisp one-dollar bills according to how long the job took and how well we'd done it, evidence, to me at least, that the world was a fair place, that we all had common cause. Unlike the ones on stately, tree-lined Kingsboro Avenue, the houses that lined our streets were modest, a mix of one- and two-family dwellings built close together. Summers, when the windows got thrown open, you could overhear your next-door neighbors' indoor conversations. Like my grandfather, many of the owners of these houses had never owned a home before. Until fairly recently they'd been renting apartments in even-more-cheek-by-jowl dwellings in less desirable parts of town, closer to the glove shops and tanneries, as well as the creek where the chemicals and dyes used in the tanning process got dumped.

For the most part, homeowners in our neighborhood did their own upkeep. Few had the wherewithal to hire professionals for tasks they could manage themselves, so on Saturday mornings they tended their own postage-stamp lawns and terraces with edge trimmers and whisper-quiet push mowers. Keeping the grounds neat was the easy part. The houses themselves were more demanding. Each spring the heavy wooden ladders came out, beasts that, when fully extended, reached all the way to the second-story roofline. Up they climbed, these men clad in threadbare, olive-drab work clothes and paint-splattered boots, metal scrapers sticking out of the hip pockets. Up under the eaves, where winter had done the most damage, they gripped the top rung of their ladders tightly and leaned out as far as they dared, scraping the curled paint and exposing the bare wood beneath. Scraping, scraping, four or five clapboards at a time, flecks of dry paint fluttering to the ground below, though they sometimes landed in the hair of boys like me who'd been stationed at the foot of the ladder to make sure it stayed secure. Gradually, I came to suspect that the real reason for our presence was to help us understand how duty bound even a modest home made you, how it owned you, even as you owned it. Finished under the eaves, those men like my grandfather would descend a few rungs, and then a few more, scraping, scraping, until they neared the bottom, where the remaining clapboards could be scraped from the ground. Then the ladder would be wrestled a few feet along the side of the house—*bang! bang! bang!* the windows rattling—and the scraping would continue. At the end of the day, rather than haul those big ladders back into the cellar, the men set them down alongside the house, no need to worry that anyone would make off with them. That sort of thing might happen in their old neighborhoods but not in this better one.

How much scraping got done during any given spring depended on how many rainy Saturdays there were. (Sundays meant church and were otherwise a day of rest.) Some years it was summer before actual painting could begin. By then, baseball season was in full swing, so a battery-powered transistor radio tuned to the Yankees game would be brought out. Once again, our neighborhood men, this time with paintbrushes sticking out of their hip pockets, ascended their ladders, even more carefully now because they were hauling up heavy cans of paint, which they secured to the top ladder rung by means of an S-hook. As before, they held on tight and leaned out as far as they dared, slapping their brushes against the dry, thirsty wood, massaging the paint in. Progress slowed when the neighbors gathered at the foot of the ladder to watch the work, offer advice and gossip. But by the end of the summer, one side of the house, maybe two if the weather had cooperated, would be restored, and the men, their faces and arms now brown from the sun, would stand with their backs against their neighbor's house to survey their accomplishment. Satisfied with a job well done, the men lowered the ladders and lugged them indoors, down into the damp cellar where they would be stowed for another year.

What did they call themselves, these proud Helwig Street / Sixth Avenue homeowners? Without exception, they thought of themselves as Americans, by which they meant assimilators, people who had decided not to live among others of their own ethnicity. Oh, sure, they might belong to the Irish or Italian American society or the Croatian Club. Their kitchen cabinets were full of recipes passed down from the old country—Sunday gravy, corn beef and cabbage, shashlik—but on Helwig Street and Sixth Avenue the idea was to ride the wave of postwar optimism that my mother believed in and my father did not. The boys who stood at the foot of those ladders were urged to do well in school so we'd maybe qualify for a New York State Regents scholarship that would allow us to go to college nearby. What was *not* given voice was this: proud as they were of the houses they tended so faithfully, men like my grandfather were also anxious about the risk they represented. What if they turned out to be bad investments? Their jobs in the glove shops and tanneries were often dangerous. What if you were injured or fell ill and couldn't make the mortgage payment? To have a house and lose it would be worse than never having one to begin with. Despite their optimism about America's future, these men were still not entirely convinced that homeownership was meant for people like them.

Gut Punch

Hence, a lifetime later, that gut punch. At first, I can't quite comprehend what I'm seeing. Every third or fourth house in my old neighborhood is now boarded up or abandoned, their postage-stamp terraces either bare or overtaken by weeds. Though there are no children in evidence, the cracked sidewalks are littered with broken toys. Some porches slope, others have been torn away completely, the front door now four feet off the ground, the house's cracked foundation visible. In another yard, a FOR SALE sign has toppled over, and no one has bothered to set it upright, because who on earth would buy a home on a street like this one? A police car sits in the driveway of a house you'd think would be condemned, but no, people are living there. A morose-looking couple is standing in the open doorway, trying to explain something to the two uniformed police officers who have been summoned there. What I'm looking at is the kind of economic devastation I read about daily in the newspaper, stories about Appalachia and the rural Midwest, where whole communities have been devastated by the opioid epidemic, where people are dying what pundits are calling deaths of despair. There are other neighborhoods in Gloversville that I wouldn't have been surprised to find in this condition, but not this one, not the one I grew up in. Earlier, on Route 29, I'd been toggling between my parents, seeing first through my father's eyes, then my mother's. Now it's my grandfather's ghost I'm confronting. Time collapses and I'm once again the boy who stood at the foot of his ladder as he dutifully scraped and painted the house he never would have purchased if he hadn't understood that, when my parents split up, my mother and I would need a place to live. His sense of duty and courage and sacrifice has come to this? It takes me a moment to realize that it's not just what I'm seeing that's shaken me to my core but also what I'm not seeing. Other than the cops and the morose-looking couple they're interviewing, the street feels deserted. Where *is* everyone? The old neighborhood of my childhood and adolescence was full of activity, people congregating on their porches, calling across the street to their neighbors, saying they were headed to the store and did we need anything. Common cause. Common purpose. People with not much money but a ton of hope. Is it today's economic devastation that has driven everyone indoors? Lack of hope for tomorrow? If these people who now live here were asked how they self-identify, would they even say they were Americans? Or would they name their political affiliation?

If my grandfather were here—and it feels like he is—I would have some serious explaining to do, because what I'm feeling at this moment, no doubt about it, is profound shame, as though I've somehow betrayed not just him but all the other good men who climbed those ladders when I was a boy, men who believed in an America that for too many is now out of reach. I would like to plead my case, to remind them that I haven't lived here in five decades, that none of this is my fault. But that would entail explaining about where I *do* live, in Portland, Maine, on Munjoy Hill, a neighborhood that once resembled this one. Indeed, lifelong Portlanders remember the Hill as being full of recent immigrants who lived in two-, three- and four-decker clapboard dwellings situated on narrow lots with tiny terraces. A friend of mine remembers being warned by his parents never to venture onto the Hill, which they considered danger-ous. Today, this same neighborhood is unaffordable to most and becoming more so with each passing year. My wife and I own a condo in a high-rise built back in the sixties at the very top of the Eastern Promenade. Our balcony has a stunning view of Portland Harbor where, directly below us, mega-yachts belonging to people who own things like professional sports teams drop anchor each summer. Nearby, there's a huge development getting ready to break ground that will offer hundreds of new condos and townhouses and luxury apartments, second and third homes that will force Portland's essential workers—firefighters, teachers, cops and service-industry folks—farther out into the hinterlands. All of this is taking place at the same time that other parts of Portland are overrun with tent cities that provide minimal shelter for the legions of people who can't make it here anymore.

The case I would like to make to my grandfather is that I'm no more to blame for any of this than I am for global warming, the pandemic, the war in Ukraine, the cesspool of social media or our politically polarized country. I'm a storyteller, not a politician. The problem is that while I may not be responsible for the growing divide between the world's haves and its have-nots, it's also true, or at least it feels true, that the world's disarray is worsening on my watch. What I'd like is to be let off the hook, to be absolved of all wrongdoing, when in truth I feel both complicit and utterly helpless. Though I live in the present, I can't help feeling that I owe an apology to both the past (the men and women of my old neighborhood, who found common cause in the promise of America) and the future (my grandchildren, to whom I'm leaving a mess beyond imagining). The rear bumper of my Mazda SUV sports a sticker of the Hungry Caterpillar that says EAT THE RICH, but what I seem to mean is EAT OTHER RICH PEOPLE, WHOSE ASSETS DWARF MY OWN. Though I've never pursued wealth for its own sake, the truth is that my long career in writing books and screenplays has been more lucrative than I ever imagined. No, I neither own a yacht nor aspire to, but when I'm sitting on my balcony high atop the

Eastern Prom in Portland, Maine, a glass of wine in hand and watching the sun go down, I'm well aware that I am literally above the fray.

On my book tour, I crossed paths on a couple occasions with my friend Ann Patchett, who was touring with her new novel *Tom Lake*. One evening, before a large crowd in Cambridge, we discussed how much more difficult it's become these days to convince ourselves that storytelling, to which we've both devoted our lives, really matters in a world that's spinning out of control, yes, on our watch. We decided on a mantra: *If it mattered before, it still does; if it doesn't now, it never did.* It's not a bad mantra. It happens to be true, actually. After the 9/11 attacks, what we desperately needed from Bruce Springsteen was a song and, as always, he delivered. The worse things get, the more suffering and injustice there are in the world, the *more* necessary art becomes. It shouldn't be necessary to repeat my mantra every single day, but damned if it isn't.

September When It Comes

The Tuesday after Labor Day, my wife and I arrive on Martha's Vineyard, where we will spend most of September. Here on the island, with our usual obligations and responsibilities temporarily on pause, our behavior will be completely, lavishly selfish. In addition to the cardboard boxes containing our electronics (laptops, a printer, tangles of cords) and multiple suitcases crammed with swimwear and other summer apparel, we've also brought to the island a bocce set, gloves and knives for shucking oysters, a couple cases of wine and, most important, an enormous canvas bag full of books. During the rest of the year my reading is directed by editors and publishers who send me advanced reader's editions of books they hope I'll read and endorse, many of them by emerging writers, which means I get to discover lots of exciting young talent long before the general public will make their acquaintance. Early in August, though, I start setting aside books I've been wanting to read over the last twelve months and haven't been able to make time for. Many of these are by eminent genre writers—think Tana French, Dennis Lehane, Louise Penny, Stephen King— who don't get their literary due because their books are just too damn much fun to read. (Our Puritan streak has never been completely eradicated; making things look easy inevitably invites disdain or dismissal. There's a reason Cary Grant never won an Oscar.) Here on the island, I'll devour two or three of these books a week, and at the end of the month I'll return home feeling as if my literary spine has been realigned.

This year we are in particular need of rest and relaxation after the book-tour grind, the absolute nadir of which took place just across Nantucket Sound on Cape Cod where, like William Henry Devereaux Jr. in *Straight Man*, I passed a kidney stone, then bled all the way from Falmouth to Chatham and back again. (My advice to all those emerging writers whose books I endorse in any given year? *Be careful what you write about.*) Given that my wife and I spend a good chunk of every September here on the Vineyard and that one of my recent novels (*Chances Are . . .*) is set there, readers might infer that we own a house here, but no, we're renters. One of the first things I do when we arrive, however, is pick up a copy of the island real estate guide so that Barbara, who has recently retired from a career in real estate, can study this year's offerings. Because we always wonder—really, we can't help ourselves—if this will be the year.

Delighted though I am to be back on the island, something feels off this year. Normally, because I first visited the Vineyard with my mother, I tend to channel her postwar optimism here. And really, doesn't the mere fact that we've arrived for yet another September suggest that she was right? And yet, for some reason, I'm out of sorts. It's as if the ghost of my father, who didn't believe that America would be a better, more just place after the war, has somehow slipped his geographical tether and hitched a ride with us on the ferry, determined to undermine our vacation. Or maybe it's Gloversville itself that's followed us here. In the month since we visited my old neighborhood, the shame I felt over its shocking economic decline has not entirely dissipated, nor has my sense of having somehow betrayed my grandfather after all the sacrifices he made for my mother and me.

It's possible, of course, that I'm overreacting. My cousin Greg and his wife, Carole, who live there, seem to have taken things in stride. Since returning home, I've thought a lot about their house on Sixth Avenue. As an adolescent I spent almost as much time there as I did on Helwig Street, and it's changed very little. The grounds, however, are unrecognizable. On the sloping front terrace and the narrow strip of lawn between the house and driveway, Carole has planted an array of bright flowers and colorful shrubs. The more expansive backyard, where there used to be a large, aboveground pool, is even more lavish in its plantings, as if the gardener were a professional whose last gig was at Versailles. I could be wrong, but I interpret what Carole has done with the property as a fierce, defiant reaction against the encroaching economic distress all around her. In the past I've been guilty of seeing her and Greg as trapped by the house they inherited from his parents, as lacking the financial wherewithal to move to some less beleaguered place. That's certainly how my mother would have understood it. But of course nothing could be further from the truth. Gloversville, this neighborhood, is their home, and it's here they've hunkered down. *They* didn't grow up with a parent who saw home as a place to escape from.

Perhaps because of how different our lived experiences have been, I continue to be fascinated by the psychological overlap that exists between my cousin and me, in particular the impulse to choose between our parents. I've always explained my own need to do so as the inevitable consequence of my own parents' failed marriage. When your mother and father agree about next to nothing, when their disagreements are deeply rooted in not just temperament but experience, it naturally follows that you yourself will end up conflicted, maybe even determined to resolve the conflict that they could not. But I've noticed that children who are the products of more successful marriages, whose parents pull in the same direction toward a shared goal, also feel that same impulse. My wife loved both her parents, but she freely admits to "choosing" her father, opting to emulate how he, not her mother, navigated the world. Greg too has chosen, I think. Despite being a college graduate and speaking, for the most part, what's commonly referred to as standard, grammatical English, I've noticed that he will sometimes channel his father, my uncle Mick, who grew up on a farm out in the sticks and was never able, despite four years of high-school English, to banish the word *ain't* from his vocabulary. "I'm lucky," Greg will say. "My kids all done good." It's his father's pride in his own children's accomplishments—how Greg and his siblings "all done good" by taking advantage of the opportunities he and my aunt Phyllis were able to provide—that I hear my cousin giving voice to. I'm not sure he's even conscious of what he's doing when he channels his father this way, but to an outsider it seems pretty clear. What's also evident is that such choices, which taken at face value might seem trivial, can trail significant consequences. It's hard to see Greg's instinctive channeling of his father as unrelated to his decision to return to Gloversville after college and make his life there. This is not to say that in different circumstances he doesn't channel his mother, as well. It just means that he and I are both haunted. Show me someone over the age of fifty who isn't.

A Finer Place

Again, be careful what you write about. Like my cousin Greg and me, Jack Griffin, the protagonist of my 2009 novel, *That Old Cape Magic,* also channels his deceased parents, two bitter midwestern academics who vacation on Cape Cod each summer, hoping (like Barbara and me on the Vineyard) that this will be the year they find a place they can afford to buy. And each summer pretty much the same thing happens. As Griffin's parents pore over their real estate guides, the listings fall into two distinct categories: *Can't Afford It* and *Wouldn't Have It as a Gift.* The problem, as they see it, is that the place they desire is, well, desirable. Lots of people want to live on the Cape, so, with demand high and supply limited, everything just keeps getting more and more expensive. Even when they have a good year (one of them getting promoted or publishing a university press book), it's never quite good enough. Less obvious to them is that with each passing year Griffin's parents become more difficult to please. What might have satisfied them a decade ago no longer does. At the heart of their conundrum, of course, is their belief in the existence of "a finer place" to begin with, as well as the implied promise that trails in its wake: *If we lived here, we'd be happy.* As a grown man Griffin knows better. Even if they'd somehow found a way to buy the Cape house they lusted after, they would never have been happy.

The idea of a finer place, where happiness is easier to imagine, was one of Mother's core tenets, and it's the reason she scrimped and saved so we could spend one short week on Martha's Vineyard the summer I was (if memory serves) ten years old. Her purpose was simple—to show me a better place than the one I knew. That way, when I was older, I wouldn't settle: for Gloversville, for Helwig Street, for Sixth Avenue. Apparently, for her purposes Saratoga, with its long boulevard lined with elegant old hotels, wasn't grand enough or, more likely, distant enough. She wouldn't have wanted me to conclude that *truly* fine places existed anywhere near where we lived. Still, why the Vineyard? The island wasn't nearly as famous then as it is now. My best guess is that she heard about it from one of the engineers she worked with in the computer room in Schenectady. They came from all over to run their programs on GE's big mainframe there. One of them probably vacationed on the island with his family and talked the place up, maybe even suggesting my mother write to the island's chamber of commerce. How crushed she must've been when the big envelope full of glossy brochures arrived and she discovered there was almost nothing we could afford, even for such a short period of time. Why else would she have chosen a remote, up-island resort in Menemsha where, upon arriving, we would be effectively marooned? Without a car (we didn't have one; my mother didn't know how to drive) we wouldn't be able to explore the island. We were also sequestered from the other guests, most of whom were quartered in the sprawling main inn, which must've been beyond our means because we were assigned one of the handful of tiny cabins midway down the sloping lawn. Each morning we made our way up the hill for breakfast in the main dining room, where we were given a bag lunch to take with us to the beach below. All meals were included, which meant that we wouldn't have ventured out even if we'd been able to. Clearly, my mother had spent her last bent farthing just getting us there. Thankfully, seeing how adrift and out of our element we were, a few of the other guests took pity on us. A young fellow offered to give me tennis lessons, and an older couple took us with them to a surf beach one afternoon so I could frolic in the waves. During cocktail hour, several of the single men there seemed interested in my mother despite the anchor she was towing.

Though it was never explicitly stated, I understood from the outset that the purpose of our coming to the island was not so much recreational as educational. What my mother wanted me to observe and appreciate wasn't so much the snazzy resort itself, or the fine cuisine of the restaurant, or even the natural beauty of the island, but rather the people we met there, how different they were from people back home, how they dressed and, especially, spoke. Nobody used the word *ain't* or said that somebody *done good*. Instead of talking over one another, they waited patiently for whoever was speaking to finish before inserting their own opinions. This was important because once we'd put Gloversville behind us for good, these would be the sorts of people I'd be associating with. Their manners were worth studying and emulating. If I learned how to dress and behave as they did, no one would ever guess where I was from. (Becoming educated, for my mother, was not unlike entering the witness protection program.)

If it appears that I'm making her out to be the same sort of snob Griffin's parents were in *That Old Cape Magic*, nothing could be further from the truth. It was their *own* escape from what they called "the mid-fucking-west" that they were deter-mined to effect. Young Griffin was simply along for the ride. By contrast, my mother did nothing without carefully calculating its impact on me. That's not to say that she didn't fall in love with the Vineyard herself or that it didn't confirm her belief in the existence of finer places where happiness was easier to imagine. But to her way of thinking, what made her enormous sacrifice worth it was the effect the island had on me. What I was glimpsing, she believed, was my own future, or rather the one she was imagining for me. In either event, she had to have been pleased with the result, because despite the brevity of our visit, the island did cast a powerful spell on me, one that didn't wear off. What tremendous vindication she must have felt nearly two decades later when one of the first things I wanted to do after getting married was show Barbara the island. Further vindication would follow when we took our young daughters there and again when they introduced the island to the men they intended to marry, letting our future sons-in-law know that this place was somehow important to the family they were marrying into.

That my mother was confident she'd accomplished her mission was evidenced by the fact that we talked very little about the island after we returned home. She seemed to feel no need to reinforce the lessons I'd learned there, about how educated people spoke and dressed and behaved. What required more or less constant reinforcement over the next eight years was the Plan. I *would* become educated. I *would* go to a university somewhere out West. To this end, we took no more expensive vacations. She continued to scrimp but now with a different goal in mind. She would put aside enough money to cover my freshman year. After that, it would be my job to excel and earn scholarships and secure other forms of financial aid. Nor, I understood, was the Plan just about us. If everything went the way it was supposed to, it would prove that her optimistic vision of postwar America was justified.

Did it work? The Plan? I've thought about this a lot over the years. Given how hard she worked and how much she sacrificed, my mother had every reason and right to feel justified by the outcome, though, as victories went, she came to understand that hers was neither complete nor entirely satisfying. Clearly, neither she nor I made the clean getaway she was hoping for. When I was a boy and we disagreed about something that mattered, she would patiently explain that I would understand when I was older. Given time, I would come to see things her way. Though she was as proud as a mother could be of my accomplishments as a writer, I'm pretty sure that my books dashed that fondest of hopes. She hadn't even wanted me to *be* a writer and tried her best to talk me out of it when I announced my intention. To her way of thinking, it was a terrible risk to take, especially for a young man with a family. (She wasn't wrong.) After all, the Plan she thought we agreed on was all about safety, security, responsibility, respectability. Otherwise, what was the point of learning a new language, a new way of dressing and speaking and behaving? The idea had always been about locating a newer, better, safer reality than the one we were leaving behind and somehow finding a way to fit in, all of which I was now blowing up. Even so, she probably would've been able to reconcile my career choice if only I'd turned out to be a different *kind* of writer, one who set his novels in some finer place, like London or Paris. In *Straight Man* why couldn't I make Hank Devereaux Jr. the chair of the English department at Princeton instead of some third-tier academic institution in dirty central Pennsylvania? Was it really necessary for me to make fun of Hank's father, a famous Ivy League scholar, the kind of man she'd so hoped I would become? What hurt her most, of course, was that I kept returning, over and over, to Mohawk and North Bath, fictionalized versions of the place we were from. Why enter the witness protection program and then tell everyone who you used to be? The only thing my doing so could possibly mean was that I'd chosen to see the world through my father's eyes, not hers. He, not she, had been right about America.

The irony, of course, is that if my father had lived to see how things worked out, he would have declared my mother, not himself, the victor. Oh, sure, I *wrote* about my hometown, but I didn't *live* there. I didn't hang out with guys like him and his friends, but with the kind of people my mother predicted I'd take up with. It's real estate on Martha's Vineyard that Barbara and I check out every September, not properties in Gloversville, or even Saratoga. Like Sully's son, Peter, in *Somebody's Fool,* my allegiances were clearly with Schuyler Springs, not North Bath.

Ashes

Though the Vineyard never lost its magic for me, it saddens me to report that it did for my mother. One summer, when Barbara was in Arizona visiting family, I took her back to the island for a long Columbus Day weekend. That late in the season, many of the up-island resorts like the one we stayed at in Menemsha were closed, so I booked us a suite in a grand old inn at the end of Water Street in Edgartown. Right from the start I knew I'd made a mistake. Rather than taking her for a stroll down memory lane and allowing her to derive pleasure from the memory of the gift she'd given me at such great cost, she was instead adrift in a frightening present. By then the anxieties that had burdened her going all the way back to Helwig Street had intensified, and now here we were in a strange place. What would happen if she and I somehow became separated?

I'd hoped that my proximity, which had a calming effect at home, would prove useful here, too, but it didn't. If we went to a gift shop, we couldn't just browse. It wasn't enough to be in the same store. We had to be in the same aisle. Indeed, we had to be studying the same object and arriving at the same conclusion about it. To me, it felt like some new, perverse manifestation of a truth I'd been dealing with ever since Barbara and I brought her to live with us—that I was all she had left. For her, the island's spell, the promise of happiness in a finer place, had been broken.

Then again, maybe not. A few years later, when I suggested it, she liked the idea of coming to rest on the island, where we could all visit her. And so, it was in Menemsha Harbor that my wife and I and our daughters and sons-in-law made good on my promise to scatter her ashes there.

Route 29 Redux

So, which of my parents was right about postwar America? Well, that's the question I've been asking over the course of ten novels, two collections of short stories and two books of essays. The answer I've come up with is both and neither. My mother was wise to be optimistic, I think, not because she was *right* to be, but because optimism, in general, is much more likely to pay dividends. As I've written elsewhere, the problem with pessimism is that while you get to be right a lot, being right seldom gets you anywhere, unless you find it satisfying to go through life saying, *I told you so.* Where my parents were both wrong, of course, was that they weren't really arguing about postwar America so much as their own place in one small corner of it. It wouldn't have occurred to them to wonder how Black veterans returning from the war might benefit or be excluded from major legislations like the GI Bill, whether they too might be able to continue their education or buy a starter home. In their defense, there weren't a lot of Black people living in my parents' particular neck of the Adirondack woods, but it's also fair to say they didn't see the ones there were and wouldn't have paused to consider how they might factor into the dispute they were having. It's also fair to say that in this respect I am very much their son. In these pages, as well as in my novels and essays and short stories, I've toggled back and forth between my mother and father, seeing the world through each of their eyes, but my attention has always remained focused on place and class, at the expense of other prisms through which our country might be viewed.

And maybe asking which of my parents was right about America is the wrong question to begin with. Perhaps better to ask who benefited from the conflict they were unable to resolve. Here, the answer is clear. The main beneficiary was me. It's not answers, or even wisdom, that begets writers. It's questions. Ask the right ones—those that resist easy answers—and you find purpose. What I hope is clear to readers of these pages is my profound gratitude to the various ghosts that haunt them, their persistence, their refusal to let go of me, to leave me in peace. If they ever did that, as a writer, at least, I would cease to exist. It's mystery that beckons us. In her song "Everyone but Me," Rosanne Cash confronts the paradox of losing her own famous parents. Now that they're gone, it seems to her that they were here "not nearly long enough," even as "it seems too long." In other words, it's not unlike Route 29 between Saratoga and Gloversville. It can last twenty minutes or a lifetime, depending on how you're measuring. Cash's advice? "Tie your shoes real tight," because "it goes by real fast."

That it does.

Part II

ART

The Lives of Others

My friend Jenny Boylan and I are both incorrigible dinner-party raconteurs who love to one-up each other with stories about our misspent youths and eccentric families. Since we're both writers, the best of these tales run the risk of theft, which is why often, as soon as the speaker's voice falls, the listener will serve notice: *You have one year to use that,* we warn, after which the story becomes fair game. Of course, these aren't so much "stories" in the literary sense as alcohol-fueled anecdotes, and often it isn't even the whole tale we covet, just its setup, perhaps, or a particularly vivid image. For instance, Jenny once made the mistake of telling me about a relative of hers whose lengthy visits were always preceded, sometimes weeks before, by the arrival of his enormous trunk; the idea so tickled my fancy that I used it as the basis for a screenplay that became the movie *Keeping Mum*. (And no, I didn't share the money.) Implicit in our agreement is a shared belief that nobody really "owns" the raw materials from which fiction is made. No doubt the fact that we're such good friends also plays a role. We share some of our best material because we know we can trust each other with intimate knowledge. When Jenny decided to transition, I was one of the first people she confided in, and I was with her when she underwent gender confirmation surgery. As a result, for the last decade or so, I've had a better window than most cis men through which to view the lives of trans women, though I've never put a trans character in one of my fictions. I take that to mean that I've voluntarily placed a limit on both what I'm willing to borrow and what I'm capable of imagining. I wouldn't argue I have no right to do either, only that I'm constrained by friendship.

But such is not always the case, even when love is involved. My mother would've hated every word of my memoir *Elsewhere*. Though I never promised not to write about her life—I had already done so obliquely in my early novels—she would have seen *Elsewhere* as a terrible betrayal. That I waited until she died to write it doesn't really matter, because other people who loved her were still alive, and I told these people a secret that she'd guarded at great cost her entire life: that she suffered from crippling anxieties, which manifested as paralyzing panic attacks that got worse over time because they went untreated. My writing *Elsewhere* meant that many of her friends and relatives wouldn't be able to remember her as she wanted them to. *Who would do such a thing?* you ask. Well, *writers* do, to some degree, pretty much every time they put pen to paper. We are, like other creators—painters, photographers, filmmakers, musicians—people who make use of whatever materials are at hand, much as carpenters use nails and wood. Without these materials, we're out of business and nothing gets made. Flannery O'Connor argued that writers' materials are humble—whatever exists in the world, whatever can be apprehended by the senses—that is, rocks and trees and lakes, and, yes, people. It's probably worth saying again: writers use people. That's inevitable and inescapable. What matters most is how we use them and for what purpose.

Take, for instance, the octogenarian nun who's the protagonist of my story "The Whore's Child." In it, Sister Ursula tells her life story to the other students in a creative writing workshop over the course of a semester: how as a child, she, the daughter of a prostitute, was taken to a convent and abandoned there; how she was made fun of relentlessly, not just by the other children but also by the nuns; how she patiently waited to be rescued by her beloved father, who had solemnly promised to fetch her as soon as he could find work. It's a cruel tale, made that much more cruel by the fact that in Sister Ursula's final workshop installment another student intuits a terrible truth that the old nun herself had never suspected—that her father, the man she'd counted on to rescue her, was her mother's pimp, his looking for work a lie. All Sister Ursula's life she's blamed her mother for things that were someone else's fault. To the father she's worshipped, she had always been expendable.

When I toured with my first story collection, also entitled *The Whore's Child*, I was both surprised and thrilled to learn how forcefully the story had landed. Sister Ursula had broken readers' hearts, much as she'd broken mine. Not so the story's other main character, the middle-aged professor who teaches that creative writing course, a novelist whose career has stalled and whose marriage is crumbling as the result of an extramarital affair. Because I too was a middle-aged novelist who back then taught creative writing, it didn't surprise me when readers wanted to know if the writer in the story was me. Was I too getting divorced? Did I think my own writing career had stalled? To such queries I had a glib reply that was at least half serious. Why, I asked those autobiography seekers, didn't they want to know if I was the nun? Because of course it was Sister

Ursula I was proudest of and to whom I felt the deepest psychic connection, though I'd never been and would never be an eighty-year-old Belgian nun. And yet I'd told her story to readers, many of whom were clearly convinced of her reality. Okay, they weren't octogenarian Belgian nuns either, at least not to my knowledge, which meant that if I got things wrong about her life in the convent I was pretty safe. Sister Ursula was only real in the peculiar way that vividly drawn fictional characters are. Readers understand them to be figments of their authors' imagination, yet somehow care about what happens to them as if they were friends or relatives. Sister Ursula limps through the first installment of her story on bloody feet, having been given shoes that were two sizes too small when she entered the convent, and her suffering from that cruelty hurt both her creator (me) and readers, most of whom, one assumes, had little or no firsthand experience of wearing shoes that are too small or of being abandoned in a convent. Despite Sister Ursula's stipulated unreality, we still share her imagined suffering. How does that work, exactly? And conversely, why doesn't an abundance of shared experience guarantee sympathy? I know more than enough about writers and college professors to render them authentically, yet it's the octogenarian Belgian nun, not the college professor, that both I and my readers feel the most affection for. Indeed, too much shared experience can impede emotional connection. Imagine, for instance, the reception "The Whore's Child" would have received if only cloistered elderly Belgian nuns had been permitted to read it. Would Sister Ursula feel real to them? Or would they laugh her out of the convent, and me along with her? Because, come on. Who is this middle-aged American writer who clearly never spent a minute inside a convent, or in a nun's habit, or probably even in Belgium? What gives him the right to intrude so arrogantly into their lives? Why doesn't he understand that Sister Ursula's story simply isn't his to tell?

The time-honored answer to this what-gives-you-the-right question is: creative imagination, which for the writer is a muscular species of empathy. *Okay, I'm not you,* the logic goes, *but if I take the time to observe you carefully, if I study how you navigate the world, if I listen to you when you speak, then in time I can begin to imagine what it feels like to be you.* Obviously, the important word here is *begin,* because employing creative imagination isn't as simple as asserting your right—obligation?—to let your imagination range freely. The further a story strays from your first- and secondhand experience (*this happened to me* or *I witnessed this happening to somebody I know*), the greater your need to narrow the ignorance gap, to make sure the details are as close to right as you can get them. Your need for a tutorial, though, should probably serve as a caution; presumably there are other writers out there for whom that gap is narrower; their own personal experience having dovetailed with your shared subject matter.

The good news is that in addition to research there are techniques at a writer's disposal that will mitigate this problem of authenticity. For instance, instead of selecting a point of view that looks through your character's eyes as the story unfolds, you can give yourself some distance by selecting an external vantage point, one that looks *at* her. Or you could use an intermediary, someone more like yourself, to interpret the story's main character, the way Conrad used Marlow, Fitzgerald used Nick Carraway, and Roth used Nathan Zuckerman. Should the day ever come when I want to write a story with a transgender protagonist, I would surely employ such a device. My friendship with Jenny Boylan simply wouldn't allow me to imply that I could convincingly walk in her shoes (or even, for that matter, stand up in them).

But if there's a serious gap between your personal experience and that of your story's protagonist—say, in age, gender, race, class, nationality, occupation—how can you gauge your chances of bridging it successfully? Do you even know enough to embark? How much additional research will you need? Will strategies like the ones noted above, together with your experience writing other stories, save you? It's impossible to know for certain, but again consider my Sister Ursula. Readers probably won't be shocked to learn that she was based on a real nun who took a workshop with me back in the eighties. Like my imagined Sister Ursula, she belonged to a dying order of nuns that the Catholic diocese was warehousing in a ramshackle old house in a sketchy part of town. A big, strong woman, she was, despite her advanced years, the youngest of the ancient nuns who lived there, and it was her job to take care of those who were in ill health. And like my Sister Ursula she made no secret of the fact that she hated her life, past and present. She'd joined the order she despised only after it became clear that life was offering her no other choice. Was she ever given a pair of too-small shoes and forced to wear them? Did she bleed into those shoes like my Sister Ursula did? Did she still limp in old age? Did she imagine burning that hated convent to the ground? I no longer remember which details were appropriated and which were invented. (Writers are free to forget what no longer matters, and they generally do. After a story of mine is published, I could be interrogated with rubber hoses about what I knew and when I knew it, but much of what was of paramount importance yesterday is blessedly gone today.) All I can say with confidence is that those cruel shoes were not stolen from Pee-wee Herman.

My point is that despite how different Sister Ursula was from me, I didn't have to make up all the story's narrative details.

I'd had the opportunity to study the real woman my character was based on. I'd read her account carefully, and after each installment she and I had an individual conference to discuss both the text and what other students had to say about it in class. Just as the narrator does in my story, I remember telling her that in a fiction writing class it was okay to make things up, even to (gasp!) lie, if the lie was in the service of a greater truth—and I observed the poor woman's reluctance to accept any of my advice. During that semester, I carefully watched how she navigated the world, how dutifully she read the other students' stories, how those stories troubled and mystified her. Even her curious and sometimes-revealing syntax ended up in my story. In other words, what I observed about the real woman closed the gap between me and my fictional nun. Sister Ursula was still eighty and I forty-five. She was a nun and I was an English professor. She European, I American; she poor, I comfortably middle class. Those differences just didn't matter quite so much. So . . . home free, right? Not exactly.

WHAT I'VE BEEN discussing is the *how* of writing a story that requires some degree of transcendence: How do you go about bridging the gap between what you know and what you don't and sometimes can't? But in the end it's the *why* that matters most. Why tell the story in the first place? Back when the nun was in my writing class, I had no idea I would ever use her. What I *did* know, as writers often do, was that the woman piqued my interest. Like most authors, I unconsciously classify everything into two categories: what might one day be of use, and everything else. It's an embarrassing habit, selfish in the extreme, but it's also a kind of artistic triage, necessary because you can't pay equal attention to everything and be an artist.

You learn, over time, to identify not so much what's important as what's important to *you*. What's likely to bear fruit and
what isn't. It would be a good decade after I taught that real-life
creative writing class before I would write the fictional one, a
decade before the elderly nun I observed so carefully without
knowing why would limp from the back of my brain to the
front and explain exactly what she meant to me.

But why did she do that? Why did I write her story and
not some other? Because I remembered so much about her?
Because what I'd learned through careful observation gave me
the confidence necessary to embark? That may be part of it.
Who doesn't want to feel confident, especially at the beginning
of a difficult endeavor? But it's also true that writers—at least
good ones—are more attracted to questions than to answers. If
knowledge (information, personal experience) were all it took
to write a good story, all artistic dilemmas would be resolved
by further research; imagination wouldn't factor in at all. What
ultimately convinces the writer to embark upon a story is not
confidence that he knows as much as he needs to. Rather he
senses a powerful bond between himself and the person (or
people) he's writing about, a bond that makes the hazardous
journey worthwhile.

When I ask why the old nun I tried to teach how to lie a
decade earlier migrated from the back of my brain to the front,
what I'm really asking is: Why was she important enough to
remember when ninety percent of my firsthand experience of
this precious life gets consigned to memory's trash heap without much thought? Different though my character and I might
be, this old woman's life somehow intersected with mine. Was
it that she spent so much of her life waiting for her father to
come back into her life, as I did after my own parents separated? Was it because she'd been mocked by cruel kids as I had

been (although no more than anyone else who's survived eighth grade)? Was it because of the lifelong, love-hate relationship with Catholicism that neither of us could purge? Was it our mutual acknowledgment of the sad truth that cruelty exists because it's pleasurable and that the very societal structures that should deter cruelty too often actually encourage it? Or did I go to the trouble of telling Sister Ursula's story because I suspected I might come to love her? Because I thought readers might as well? Because her story might both entertain and instruct them? Make them feel less alone in the world than Sister Ursula herself did?

Readers might also ask what kind of responsibility I felt to the real woman who inspired my Sister Ursula. Did I ask her permission to use the raw materials of her story to write mine? No, I didn't. For one thing I'd moved fifteen hundred miles away by then and for another I had no reason to believe she was still alive. Honestly, though, it wouldn't have mattered. The real nun, whom I remember with great affection, inspired but was not my fictional Sister Ursula. Okay, I'll say it again. Writers use people.

In the end we tell stories because we must. And the real source of that *must* isn't talent or knowledge or the authenticity that derives from research and lived experience. It's mystery. What we *don't* understand is what beckons to us. When I began writing *Elsewhere*, everything felt cloaked, especially the book's strange urgency. I was deep in a new novel and having an absolute blast when I first became aware of *Elsewhere*'s gravitational pull, and I wanted nothing more than to ignore it. Why in the world should I put aside a book that was so much fun to write for another that promised little but heartache? The story's imperative seemed to hint at some unfinished business between my mother and me, but how could that be the case? Hers had been a difficult life, and she was finally at rest. Why disturb it? I assumed the book would be about how different our temperaments had been and how that had resulted in a grinding, decades-long contest of wills. She believed that many of the crushing anxieties she was prey to might have been alleviated if only I'd been willing to take her side in matters both large and small, to assure her that she was right, even, especially, when I knew she wasn't. Why couldn't I just pretend? Was that so much to ask? Why were we so often, so intractably, at odds? She knew we loved each other, so it wasn't that. What was she missing? But here's the thing: instead of being a book about how different my mother and I were, *Elsewhere* turned out to be about how frighteningly similar we'd always been. The tractor beam of *must* that demanded I set aside my novel had nothing to do with what I understood and everything to do with what I'd stubbornly refused to grasp. This was the unfinished business I'd sensed but couldn't articulate. In the end, a writer's sense of *must* is the creative imagination's moral imperative, urging us to do *this*, not *that*. When we ignore it, our core mission is compromised. Our inability to explain it, even to ourselves, doesn't and shouldn't diminish its power.

The primary obstacle to imagination isn't lack of knowledge or lived experience. More often, it's simply our need to get over ourselves. I came to storytelling late, and like many writers, painters, musicians and other artists, I fell in love with the process long before I was any good at it. As an English major in college, I'd begun to understand why I'd always loved to read. Getting lost in a good story is an antidote to self-consciousness. But writing stories, it turned out, was even more rewarding. I'd always wanted to be a better person than I knew myself to be, and here was a pursuit that might actually help me achieve this goal. Deciding to become a writer had very little to do with whether I might one day exhibit any talent. The activity was its own reward. I no longer felt quite so trapped. *Yes, I'm me,* I remember thinking. *But for a time, I can also be you.*

EXCEPT.

Earlier this year, when I mentioned to my elder daughter, Emily, a bookseller, that I meant to write an essay defending the creative imagination, its moral urgency, she cringed, then posed an interesting hypothetical. What if the same mysterious force that made me set aside my novel for a memoir showed up again with a brand-new, even-more-suspect project? Suppose I felt a strong imperative to write a novel about what it feels like to be a Black man in America? *Oh, come on,* you say? Why would a seventy-year-old white writer suddenly be visited by this particular sense of *must*? A fair question—except, well, it happens.

Consider the case of John Howard Griffin, a writer who, back in the fifties, darkened his skin in order to (in his own words) "become a negro." The book he wrote about his experience traveling through the Jim Crow South was the huge bestseller *Black Like Me,* and despite the book's extraordinary sales, there's little evidence of opportunism in its writing or publication (both Griffin and his publisher envisioned a small, mostly scholarly readership). Apparently, the author just needed to know, firsthand, what it felt like to navigate the South as a Black man. It could be argued that even with the best of intentions, he was still the wrong person to tell that particular story. But it could also be argued, given the historical context, that the wrong man was actually the right one. After all, Black authors had been writing about the corrosive effects of racism for decades, and white readers turned a deaf ear until one of "their own" chimed in. What Griffin did not do, however, is as interesting as what he did. Despite being a fiction writer, he didn't use his lived experience to write a novel. Rather *Black Like Me* was a kind of literary hybrid, a "nonfiction novel" that predated Capote and Mailer. Griffin's decision not to fictionalize his experience suggests he believed that being treated like a Black man didn't mean he could imagine what it would've been like to be born Black and to live as a Black man over a lifetime. After the publication of *Black Like Me,* he became friends with Martin Luther King Jr., Dick Gregory and other prominent members of the civil rights movement, but as time passed, Griffin grew increasingly uncomfortable talking about his famous book. There were other, more authentic voices, he decided, and they deserved the microphone more than he did.

But none of this negates the moral imperative Griffin must have felt to undertake such a radical experiment. Which begs an obvious question: What is a writer to do with that powerful feeling of *must* when the project it urges will strike others not as a moral imperative but rather as immoral opportunism? Because even if we acknowledge the power of the creative imagination, only a fool would ignore its hazards. My daughter reminded me that nobody ever gets everything right, and when it comes time for me to turn in my novel about what it feels like to be a Black man in America, the manuscript will likely be read only by white folks. Roughly eighty percent of the people in publishing in this country are white. My editor will likely be white, and so will my copy editor. The sales, marketing and publicity teams will also be white, as will the reps who pitch my novel to bookstore owners, most of whom will be white, too. Which means it's pretty unlikely that the mistakes I was hoping to avoid will be caught and corrected before the book goes to press. When I go out in public and give readers a big, confident smile (one imagines Al Jolson, seeing *The Jazz Singer* on the big screen and thinking, *Nailed it!*), no one will be smiling back. How will I respond when I'm told by people who know better that I didn't, in fact, nail it? Will I be sore, having tried my best? Ashamed? (What on earth was I thinking?) Resentful that so few people understand how hard it is to write even a deeply flawed book? But in the end, it's not about my embarrassment. It's about my doing a disservice to people who deserve better.

Nor is that all. What if, based on my track record as a best-selling author, my publisher has advanced me a large sum to write this novel that turns out, despite my best efforts, to be full of inaccuracies? Doesn't the money given to me diminish the opportunity for an emerging Black author with more authentic experience who's trying to sell his debut novel on the same subject? How would I feel about being complicit in the silencing of that other voice? (Not great.) Doesn't this in fact happen all too often? (No doubt in my mind.) Yes, we can argue that the ranks of authors today are more diverse than ever before, and that these new voices are finding more and more success, but until the publishing industry itself becomes more diverse, can we really pretend the playing field is level? (We cannot.) And have I really stopped to consider (did Al Jolson?) how under-represented communities are harmed by inauthentic representations like mine? (Ouch. Apparently not.)

When writers like me (older, white, male), who were taught that literary imagination was our stock-in-trade, leap to its defense, we don't always realize what those impassioned defenses sound like to younger writers who are emerging into a very different publishing reality. When I broke in, there were more publishers to submit our books to, and that competition led to larger advances. Back then, there was no Big Tech devaluing print books, not to mention digital piracy. Nor was the Internet chipping away at our attention spans with clickbait. Newspapers were still healthy enough to have book review sections. Authors of important, serious midlist books understood that while they probably weren't going to make fortunes, at least they had real careers, as did long-form journalists. Even younger writers got book tours, not because tours resulted in huge sales, but rather because publishers back then were playing a longer game. Introducing and growing new talent was crucial to their own futures. And only a few of those publishers were owned by conglomerates that also sold televisions and cars and refrigerators (and expected books to yield similar profit margins).

Considering all this, can today's emerging writers really be blamed for concluding that they're late to the party, that those of us who got there first have grazed the buffet table, drunk all the champagne and then ensconced ourselves in the comfortable chairs from which we can't seem to stop banging on about the creative imagination and how all writers should be unfettered in its use? To them it must seem as though our real goal is to extend the many privileges we've gotten used to and now regard as our due. What choice do they have but to call us out, to turn the discussion to ownership, to argue not just that certain stories but also the very materials out of which stories are made, belong to "people like me," not "people like you?" Okay, I get all that and sympathize, but it's also worth pointing out that ownership shifts the discussion from art to commerce, and these have always been at odds. Indeed, we seldom get really angry until money enters the equation. Yes, cultural appropriation is a serious issue, but books that garner ten-thousand-dollar advances and have initial print runs of eight thousand copies seldom spark serious outrage, even when they're thoroughly botched jobs. The heated debate over the literary merits of *American Dirt,* a novel by a white woman about a Mexican bookseller fleeing a cartel, was no doubt a necessary one for the industry, but it was the book's seven-figure advance and aggressive marketing campaign that caused battle lines to be drawn and invective hurled.

Lost in the resulting tumult, I think, is how much time we spend documenting the literary imagination's numerous limitations when we might be extolling its triumphs. Books are flawed because their authors are. Yes, we're beckoned by mystery and the need to understand, but also by money and fame. Shoddy work often pays better than genuine craftsmanship, arrogance better than humility, speed better than accuracy. It may be true that even when we make a good-faith effort to imagine what it feels like to be people very different from ourselves, we still fail far more often than we succeed. But what's more important? Our numerous failures, or those rarer occasions when we beat the odds and somehow manage to get it right? Because when we do, the results can be truly glorious, and then identity politics fall away. Take Rebecca Makkai's recent novel *The Great Believers*. Was that story about a generation of gay men lost to the AIDS epidemic really a straight woman's to tell? How dare she? But seriously, who, having read the novel, would want to make that case? (Fair warning, if you do, don't make it around me.) Don't we want to hold up books that represent genuine triumphs of imagination and say, *This, right here, is what we're after*? What's more important for young writers to learn? That moral imagination has its limits? Or that its judicious use, and the courage needed to employ it, can make us better artists (and, yes, better people)? If I turn away from a story, should it be because someone else has told me it's taboo, or because after my first draft I've reluctantly concluded that I'm not up to this particular task? There's no reason I shouldn't reserve the right to put a transgender character in a story at some point in the future, provided I acknowledge the moral responsibility that would trail in its wake. I would have to examine my motives, because in addition to (hopefully) making art, I would also (hopefully) be making money. I'd have to be willing to admit defeat and pull the plug should it become clear that the book I'm writing was misbegotten, even if that realization comes after years of hard work. I would owe my friend Jenny and all trans people that much.

I know—of course I do—that I can't really be a Black man any more than I can really be a nun. But why constrain imagination, the very thing that helps us get over ourselves? Are artists really supposed to stay in their lanes? Those who argue that lived experience is the only legitimate source of authenticity, the only valid test of ownership, may provide a necessary corrective to arrogance and opportunism, but such proscription inevitably leads to timidity, and great art has always demanded courage. Surely we can agree on that much. Okay, granted, it's not possible to be somebody else. We're stuck with who we are. But this only means that when we pretend otherwise, both as readers and writers, we're playing a very important, very serious game. We can't *be* somebody else, but we have to try.

The Future

Butch and Sundance

The movie begins in sepia tones, with a scratchy, mock newsreel of the Hole in the Wall Gang robbing a train. "They're all dead now," we're informed in a narration rectangle, "but once they ruled the West." When the clicking newsreel finishes, the grainy quality of the video disappears, but the sepia remains. Now we see Butch Cassidy (Paul Newman) casing a fortresslike bank. Entering moments before it's due to close, Butch registers all the changes that have been introduced since the last time he was there: armed guards, buzzers, alarms, bars on all the windows, an imposing new vault. Butch is clearly the Hole in the Wall Gang's planner and detail man, the brains of the outfit. Indeed, he believes himself to be a man of "vision" and what he sees there in the bank is that "everything's changed." Robberies will require more planning now. As they make their way back to Hole in the Wall, Butch explains to the Sundance Kid that the future isn't in America, where the gold rush is over, but rather in Bolivia, where gold, silver and tin are everywhere being extracted from the earth, and the payrolls are so heavy they'd strain themselves stealing 'em. Sundance, the gang's enforcer by virtue of his steely gaze and lightning-quick draw, has his doubts, perhaps because Butch seems none too sure where Bolivia actually is, and he gently mocks his friend's smarts, as well as, we suspect, the value of intelligence in general. "You just keep thinkin', Butch," he chortles. "That's what you're good at."

Everything's Changed

Or anyway that's what it felt like. First the pandemic, then a string of other disruptions—the murder of George Floyd, the Black Lives Matter protests, Donald Trump's attempts to overturn a free and fair election, culminating in the January 6 insurrection. All of this would change us, because how could it not? When lockdown ended and we regarded ourselves in the mirror, who exactly would be staring back at us?

In retrospect, that seems to be the one thing we needn't have worried about. Yes, many of those on the front lines—doctors and nurses in hospitals, police on the steps of the Capitol—emerged as if from a war zone: shell-shocked, dazed, traumatized. But most of us stayed pretty much in character throughout the ordeal. Kind people remained kind, angry people angry. If anything, we became more ourselves, not less. That was certainly true in my own case. Sidelined by my age (early seventies) and occupation (it's hard to argue that writers are essential workers), I basically read and wrote myself through the pandemic, though, as Butch observed, everything required more planning now. I shopped early in the morning with people my own age, planned meals four or five days in advance to eliminate unnecessary trips to the store. I tried to be safe, to keep others safe. In the end, lockdown had a clarifying effect. Like a lot of people, I discovered what was essential to my happiness and sense of purpose, as well as what I could easily live without. When the various disruptions came to an end, I would make some changes. Less self-promotion. Fewer personal appearances. More attention to family and friends. If outside forces could so disrupt our lives, why not disrupt those lives ourselves, change their trajectory for the better? But, of course, that's pretty much what Butch and Sundance tried to do by moving their operation to Bolivia. Apparently making changes is not the same as changing. Maybe that's the scariest thing about major disruptions—everything changes but us.

Escape

Unlike many people, I watched relatively little TV during the pandemic for the simple reason that it didn't distract me from reality as thoroughly as I might've hoped. The more realistic the show was, the more it would remind me of the realities I was seeking distraction from. What I had in mind was something reassuring. My wife, too, was in search of comfort, which, for her, was to be found in sitcoms that dated back to the early years of our marriage—*The Mary Tyler Moore Show*, both Bob Newhart shows, Carol Burnett. She'd fall asleep mid-episode, her iPad dutifully churning eighties dialogue into the fabric of her dreams. For reasons I didn't fully understand at the time, I dove into an even-deeper past, streaming the old Saturday afternoon matinees of my adolescence, as if in search of the boy I'd been. That boy had yearned for a life of adventure in a time machine or in the land of the Cyclops or at the center of the earth, any place that was not the decaying mill town in upstate New York where he spent his days. How, I wondered, had that boy become *me*, an aging writer who's spent most of his adult life writing stories set in the very place that boy was trying to escape? His life, I reflected, had been disrupted by education. My mother made clear from a very young age that I would go to college, and so I did, earning not just an undergraduate degree but several graduate ones. Had I not done this, I likely would have been drafted and sent to Vietnam (speaking of disruptions).

It was when I expanded my search for comfort that I came upon *Butch Cassidy and the Sundance Kid,* a movie I'd seen so many times that I'd be able to speak many of its famous lines ("Who are those guys?") before the characters did. And, yes, it *was* comforting . . . for about twenty minutes. Then it dawned on me what this movie I knew so well was actually about. I sat up straight.

Horses

Though Butch's "vision" doesn't allow him to see into the future, he has a pretty good read on the present. Yes, things *are* different now, but the inference he draws from this—that robbing trains and banks just requires more careful planning and a few extra sticks of dynamite—is not unreasonable, nor does his optimism appear unwarranted. After all, the Hole in the Wall Gang has had things pretty much their own way (they once ruled the West) and local law enforcement appears beyond clueless. Seated on the balcony of a brothel, pleasantly drunk, their feet up on the railing, Butch and Sundance revel in the street scene below, where the town's oblivious marshal tries in vain to raise a posse to pursue them. Who *wouldn't* be confident? Ironically, it's in this same scene that the real existential threat is introduced when the sheriff is joined by a traveling salesman hawking what he claims is "the future": a bicycle. "The horse," he declares, "is dead."

And there is the disruption in a nutshell: the horse is being replaced by the wheel. Butch may be right about the American gold rush being over, but in the grand scheme of things that's far less consequential than the fact that the entire West is being crisscrossed by railroads, and horses, as transportation, are everywhere being replaced by wheels. In cities back East, roads are already paved, and before long they will be in the West as well. In less than two decades horse-drawn carriages will be outnumbered by automobiles, which Bonnie Parker and Clyde Barrow, the next generation of bank robbers, will use to flee the police. Can we blame Butch and Sundance for being unable to foresee such changes? As Ezra Klein has written, "There is no more profound human bias than the expectation that tomorrow will be like today." It's also interesting to note that if the task at hand is to imagine a world where wheels are everywhere and horses nowhere (or nowhere that matters to men like them), imagining something *out* of existence proves the more difficult task. In the movie's final act, Butch and Sundance's bloody end is heralded by a mule, whose branded flank identifies its owner as the nearby mine whose payroll they've just robbed. Badly wounded and surrounded by an entire regiment of the Bolivian army, Butch tells Sundance that they should go next to Australia. Why? Well, for one thing, English is spoken there. They wouldn't be immediately recognizable as foreigners. The banks are ripe and luscious. But best of all: *they've got horses*.

Give Butch this much credit, though. He may be blind to the real threat, but he does seem to sense its proximity, and he responds by suggesting to Sundance that maybe the time has come for them to try something different: they could join the army and fight the Spanish. In other words, faced with a disruption they don't understand, they could opt to disrupt their own lives. After all, their particular skill set might dovetail nicely with what a war would demand, and for once they wouldn't be at odds with the law. The idea appeals to Butch for personal reasons, as well. There on the balcony of the brothel, he confesses that when he was younger he always thought he might grow up to be some sort of hero. "Too late for that," Sundance scoffs, but the scene turns poignant, with both men revealing, apparently for the first time, their real names (Robert LeRoy Parker and Harry Longabaugh) and just how far they've strayed from the path they meant to follow. It's a sad, lovely moment, a reckoning, of sorts. Whatever happens to them, they're complicit in their destiny.

The moment can't last, of course. "You just keep thinkin', Butch," Sundance mocks, good-naturedly. "That's what you're good at."

Planning

My parents knew something about disruption. Seeing one on the horizon, they made a plan. My father would enlist in the army early in the hope of completing his military service before America entered the war. My mother, anxious to travel, would become a camp follower, have some fun down south, and when my father mustered out, they'd get married, return home to upstate New York and start a family. The only part of the plan that came to fruition was that they got married right before he shipped overseas. By the time he returned, a bona fide war hero, he was a changed man. Given how spectacularly the last one had failed, he was all done making plans. My mother, a natural planner, was not. They would buy a small starter home, she decided, take advantage of the GI Bill, build a future. Yes, their lives had been brutally disrupted by the war and much had changed, but to her way of thinking, most of those changes were for the better. The America she envisioned would be more open to those with aspirations, and she was nothing if not aspirational. She and my father would take charge of their lives, reassert their agency.

My father's reaction to all this was not unlike the Sundance Kid's: *You just keep thinking, Jean. That's what you're good at.* You want to make God laugh? Tell him your plans. Nor did he share my mother's optimism about America changing that much after the war. The way he saw it, his name still ended in a vowel, which meant he wouldn't be standing on one leg awaiting an invitation to join the country club. Nor did he really feel like a war hero. He'd simply been lucky. Somehow, he'd managed not to get killed. But he knew better than to believe that it was because he was a better soldier than all those men who died. His own plan, if you could call it that, was henceforth to stay out of the line of fire. He would keep his head down, find the sort of job that required a strong back and the ability to put one foot in front of the other. That's how he'd made it from Utah Beach to Berlin, and he figured if the strategy worked there, it stood a reasonable chance of working in Gloversville, New York. At the end of the day there'd be a barstool and he'd settle onto it comfortably and remain right there for last call. All of which is to say that both my parents stayed in character—my mother continuing to make plans that never quite panned out, especially for her (though they often did for me); my father refusing to think about tomorrow until it arrived, if then.

But, of course, having no plan is a plan.

Woodcock

Okay, but what *should* they have done? Even with the benefit of hindsight, it's not entirely clear. If anything, the film suggests that Butch and Sundance are just fundamentally screwed. That's the view expressed by Ray Bledsoe, the sheriff they go to see in hopes that he'll be able to pull some strings and get them into the army. "Don't you *get* that?" Ray asks them in slack-jawed disbelief. "It's *over*. Your times is *over!*" The old man recognizes their strengths—Butch's charm, Sundance's quick draw—but he also understands what they don't, that in their new reality these will be of little use. "You're gonna die bloody," Ray predicts. "All you can do is choose where." The fact that this is indeed what happens makes their destiny appear inevitable, but is it? If Bledsoe can see the future so clearly, why can't they? When the traveling salesman proclaims that the horse is dead, why doesn't Butch, who claims to be a man of vision, take that possibility more seriously?

One reason might be that the salesman was, well, *selling* something, so . . . caveat emptor, especially when he's so recognizably a huckster and what's being sold is the future. But again, it's never easy to imagine a world that's radically different from the one we presently inhabit. Intellectually, we understand that things will change, but experience teaches us that most change occurs incrementally. We tell ourselves that we'll have plenty of time to sort things out, to gather and analyze data that will provide the clarity we presently lack. Indeed, it's because change mostly *does* happen slowly that we're so often unprepared for when it unexpectedly picks up speed and gathers momentum, data and clarity lagging in its wake. Suddenly, the time to act is yesterday, not today, because tomorrow is already here. But it's also worth remembering that Butch does not ignore the bicycle. In fact, he shows up at Etta Place's house riding one the very next morning, apparently willing to try the future on for size. Despite Burt Bacharach's ebullient lyrics, the famous "Raindrops Keep Fallin' on My Head" montage that follows only confirms what we already know—that for Butch, Sundance and Etta the future will not be a great fit. Butch's acrobatic tricks on the bike not only mock its utility but end in accident and minor injury. Still, can we really blame Butch for using the contraption as a goof? More to the point, what good would glimpsing the future actually do? If the Hole in the Wall Gang is fundamentally screwed, what good is prescience? If American workers had recognized that globalization would result in the outsourcing of millions of jobs overseas, what could they have done to stop that from happening? If they'd understood how many jobs would be lost to robotics, both here and abroad, how could those losses have been prevented? Do we really need a crystal ball to predict that artificial intelligence will result in many thousands—maybe even millions—more job losses? That it will significantly, if not totally, reshape society?

The movie also demonstrates that once everything has changed, it does little good to complain. "That's bad business!" Butch exclaims when the question he asked earlier—"Who are those guys?"—is finally answered. According to the newspapers, Mr. E. H. Harriman of the Union Pacific Railroad has put together an elite posse to hunt down and eradicate the Hole in the Wall Gang. To Butch, this makes no economic sense. The posse has to be costing Harriman more than the gang ever stole to begin with. "If he'd just pay me what he's spending to make me stop robbing him, I'd stop robbing him." Harriman would have no trouble explaining his "business" decision if he were so inclined, but of course he isn't. Guys like Butch and Sundance (and like American workers whose jobs were outsourced overseas or lost to robotics) never get to meet the men who render their lives irrelevant. Their only contact with men like Harriman is through their minions, like Woodcock, whose unenviable job is to ride inside the boxcar where the safe is housed. Given explicit instructions not to open the door, all Woodcock can provide by way of explanation for his refusal to do so is to repeat that he works for Mr. E. H. Harriman of the Union Pacific Railroad, who forbids it. Perhaps because they are being ground under the same capitalist boot, Butch and Woodcock seem to like each other. Woodcock assures Butch that if the money were his, there's nobody he'd rather have steal it. But the money is *not* his. It belongs to Mr. E. H. Harriman, who "trusts" him not to open the door. "You think he'd get himself killed for *you*?" Butch asks, not unreasonably, but Woodcock remains resolute. He's Labor, and if he opens the door, he'll lose not only his employer's trust but also his job. He and Butch may be natural allies, but Capital makes sure they're on opposite sides.

The Face of Change

It's not just that intimations of the future often come to us coded, like oracles. They can also shape-shift right before our eyes. One of the more significant disruptions of my life as a writer (as well as my daughter's, as a bookseller) was the emergence of Amazon, which for years was taken about as seriously as Butch takes the bicycle. In the mid-1990s, independent bookstores were far more worried about being put out of business by juggernaut big-box stores like Barnes & Noble and Borders. Amazon wasn't even a blip on their radar. Year after year the company posted the kind of huge losses that were thought to be unsustainable. It was tempting to treat the online business model as a goof. Okay, the eerie calm of the company's owner probably should've been a tip-off, but again, even if we'd been more prescient, what exactly was to be done? Amazon only captured the attention of writers, publishers and bookstore

owners after e-books, digital readers and other digital enter-
tainments were introduced, further disruptions that Amazon
was perfectly positioned to take advantage of. Just that quickly
the company was no longer a goof. What if, as some were
claiming, the physical book, like the horse, was dead? What if
the time to act was yesterday, because tomorrow was already
here?

Well, we thought, at least we finally knew what we were up
against. Amazon intended to disrupt the lives of authors, publishers and booksellers by cornering the book market. Except,
no, it soon became apparent that this was only the tip of the
iceberg. Amazon meant to corner *all of retail*, to become "the
everything store." Except, hold on, that didn't seem quite right,
either. Maybe, we considered, our heads spinning, their real
goal was cloud computing. If true, then maybe their objectives
were more closely aligned with other tech giants. What they
were *really* after was information about us so they could sell to
us more efficiently. Unless of course what they wanted was the
unthinkable—to in some sense own *us*.

Okay, but no need to hyperventilate, right? After all, the
worst didn't happen. Independent bookstores like my daughter's in Portland, Maine, not only survived but staged something of a comeback. Data eventually did arrive and with it
some helpful analysis. It turned out there was a sweet spot for
brick-and-mortar bookstores, the right amount of square foot-
age and stock, a deeper relationship between the store itself
and the community it served. Yes, Borders went belly-up, but
Barnes & Noble survived, its new CEO deftly tinkering with
this and mending that. The printed book proved more resilient
than expected. People grew weary of screens. Publishers con-
solidated in the hopes of combating whatever Amazon hurled
at them next and actually benefited from the pandemic, which

gave people more time and inclination to read. Writers like me—sent home and told to stay there—churned out not only books and stories and essays but also movies, TV shows, other "content." In other words, we adapted. We navigated our new reality and somehow came out . . . well, not on top, exactly, but somehow . . . what? Wiser?

Well, that's one way to look at it. The other is to recognize that what we did was not so different from what Butch did when he visited that bank and saw how much had changed. Like him, we paid careful attention to those changes, understood that things would be more difficult now and played our cards smarter. Like my father in the Second World War, we somehow managed not to die. We kept our heads down, tried to stay out of the line of fire. We put one foot in front of the other and continued moving forward. We showed character. Surely that counted as some sort of victory, didn't it?

Unless, of course, we've simply been granted a stay of execution. Unless, for reasons of their own, the forces of capitalism have decided that, at least for the moment, we're worth more alive than dead. Hard to know for sure, though, because really . . . who *are* these guys?

Beauty

One thing is clear, or should be. When everything changes, the only way out is through. There's just no going back to the way things were. The task of moving forward is made immeasurably more difficult, however, by those who would convince us otherwise, that it's possible to turn back the clock and return to a world we understood and preferred. It would be nice if we could, though, wouldn't it? "What happened to the old bank?" Butch asks one of the armed guards on his way out the door. "It was beautiful." "People kept robbing it," he's told, to which Butch responds, "That's a small price to pay for beauty." In previous viewings of the film, I always thought of this as a throwaway line, funny and perfectly in character for a man who robs banks for a living, intended to grab an easy laugh but not to carry the weight of truth. But as we know, comedy can be serious business; only when we take a step back does the movie come into focus as a thoughtful study of disruption, one that raises important questions about technology and capitalism, as well as human nature. Even better, the laughs—and there are a lot of them—make the whole thing feel effortless, which is why we're likely to gloss over Butch's seemingly offhanded remark about beauty. But the past *can* appear beautiful when the present turns grim, especially if you were more prosperous then, if you had fewer worries and were more hopeful about the future, if you could tell yourself that the work you did mattered, if it allowed you to feel like you were part of the fabric of society.

As I've written here and elsewhere, my father took pride in the work he did, first as a laborer on road construction crews and later as a union plumber. Like Sully in *Nobody's Fool*, he took particular satisfaction in doing the kinds of nasty jobs that made other men queasy. Nobody enjoys standing knee-deep in raw sewage in ninety-degree heat, and nobody who's willing to do such work gets rich from it, but that doesn't make the work any less necessary. And down the road, long after the nauseating experience itself has receded into memory, you can point with pride to the thing you helped build, even if nobody knows the part you played, even if your name isn't E. H. Harriman and nobody calls you "mister," even if, when asked, Mr. E. H. Harriman claims *he* built it. What chafes you worse than the poor pay you get for hard physical labor is the low esteem in which you are sometimes held because you have only a high-school education and you work with your hands, and what has to sting even worse than *that* is to lose your work because somebody on the other side of the globe is willing to do it cheaper, which robs you not only of a paycheck but your sense of self-worth. You also suspect that if Mr. E. H. Harriman regrets anything, it's probably that he didn't outsource your ass sooner. So, when somebody tells you they can turn back the clock and you can have your old job back, that coal mining is *not* dead in West Virginia, that the paper mill that employed half your town will someday reopen, that the glove shop your grandfather helped unionize will return one day, *of course* you want to believe it. Who wants to be told, as Butch and Sundance were, that "It's *over*. Don't you get that? Your times is *done*!"

Except it is over, and they are done, whether you get it or not.

The Shape I'm In

How quickly beauty can turn ugly. When the message finally lands that "your times is done," it's just human nature to look around for someone to blame. James McMurtry puts this human need to assign blame under a microscope in his 2005 song, "We Can't Make It Here," which begins with a Vietnam veteran parked in the left-turn lane and holding up a cardboard sign, "the flag on his wheelchair flapping in the breeze." More like him are on the way, we're told, thanks to the "Mideast war." Up the street, the textile mill that provided the unnamed town's employment now sits empty: "they turned us out and they closed the doors." Why? Because "we can't make it here anymore." That line, of course, has a powerful dual meaning. It's no longer possible to make it financially in this town, and others like it all over America, because the things that were once made here are now made elsewhere. The song's narrator works in the Walmart stocking shirts manufactured in Singapore that were once made "here." Someone's to blame, but who? "Should I hate a people for the shade of their skin," the narrator asks rhetorically, "or the shape of their eyes or the shape I'm in? Should I hate 'em for having our jobs today? No, I hate the men sent the jobs away." McMurtry's narrator imagines those men "all lily white and squeaky clean. They've never known want, they'll never know need. Their shit don't stink and their kids won't bleed." And as with Mr. E. H. Harriman, they're not even around to "look us in the eye."

Alas, unbridled capitalism is an abstraction, and its victims often prefer to take out their anger on folks close to hand. And as we often see in times of disruption, many are all too willing to hate people for the shade of their skin or the shape of their eyes.

Caveat Emptor

If "buyer beware" is sound advice when someone tries to sell you the future, it's even-better advice when it's the past they're selling. Victims of disruption are prone not just to anger but also to nostalgia, convinced that the way out is not through but rather back. Wouldn't it be better, they reason, to return to, say, the 1950s, when America was simpler? Back then you could spend your whole life working for a company like General Electric, as my mother did until, in her fifties, she headed west in a desperate and ill-advised attempt to start over, to disrupt her own life, alter its trajectory, a quest that would ultimately break her spirit. Who did *she* fault? For a time, during the first Reagan term, she flirted with blaming others for the shape she was in, and, yes, she did long to return to the postwar America that got her hopes up, an America she understood and loved. But in the end she blamed herself, as she'd been taught to do. I suspect it was the Catholicism she imagined having jettisoned long ago that required her to take responsibility for all those plans that never worked out because of the magical thinking required to set them in motion.

The old bank was beautiful? Maybe, but its times, like the Hole in the Wall Gang's, were done.

The Gilded Age

Why, though? Why must your times be done? Because you don't have the skills that happen to be in demand? That's part of it, but Ray Bledsoe has a pithier explanation. "You're two-bit outlaws!" he reminds Butch and Sundance, which at first glance seems to suggest that, in the end, it all comes down to their being on the wrong side of the law. If they could just get on the right side of it, things might just work out. But listen to how Ray delivers that venomous line. *Two-bit* outlaws. The point he's making isn't really that Butch and Sundance are on the wrong side of the law or that Ray himself is on the right side. Their problem isn't that they're outlaws at all; it's that they're cheap. (Is there any doubt that Ray would consider himself a two-bit sheriff compared with the men who make up the elite posse that dogs Butch and Sundance so relentlessly?) Until she goes to Bolivia with Butch and Sundance, Etta Place has been on the right side of the law her whole life, and it does her about as much good as it's done Woodcock. Isn't she, too, just fundamentally screwed? Explaining why she's willing to tag along with Butch and Sundance, she says, "I'm twenty-six and single and a schoolteacher and that's the bottom of the pit." Her problem is the same as theirs. She doesn't matter.

It may not look like it until all three arrive in New York, but *Butch Cassidy and the Sundance Kid* is a Gilded Age tale, and it makes abundantly clear that to succeed at thievery, you need to be not a robber but a "robber baron." You need to be like Andrew Carnegie, Cornelius Vanderbilt, John D. Rockefeller, Jay Gould and J. P. Morgan, men famous for their ruthlessness and lack of ethics. Economic might, which ensures that the law will be on your side, makes right. There's no such thing as fair play. Morality has nothing to do with it.

The Money Is Ours

Right and wrong may not matter to robber barons, but it often does matter to the people they rob, even to "two-bit outlaws" like Butch and Sundance. In Bolivia, still not terribly adept at gauging which threats are existential but correctly sensing that the noose around their necks is tightening, Butch catches a glimpse of a man wearing a white skimmer and concludes that Joe LeFors, the sheriff who pursued them back in the States, has followed them to South America. If they continue to steal mining payrolls, Butch reasons, they will eventually get caught. Still a thinker, he quickly devises a plan. They'll get on the right side of the law by signing up to guard the very payrolls they've been robbing. Unfortunately, they're not the only bandits on the scene, and when the payroll they've been hired to guard is robbed and their employer killed, a showdown with the bandits results. "Tell them the money isn't ours," Sundance instructs Butch, who does his best to convey this in his primitive Spanish. The Bolivians couldn't agree more. The dinero *doesn't* belong to Butch and Sundance. The dinero is *theirs*. Moments later they all lie dead. "Well," says Sundance, sickened by what they've done, "we've gone straight." Both they and we now understand what that means for men who are robbers but *not* robber barons.

But their circumstance remains unaltered. "Everybody needs money," Danny DeVito's character says in the crime thriller *Heist*. "That's why they *call* it money." It's a glorious non sequitur that begs to be understood, because it's at the center of the eternal conflict between capital and labor, as well as the root of income inequality. A decade after the events of *Butch Cassidy and the Sundance Kid,* another technological disruption—the industrialization of American textiles—will result in a violent labor dispute in Lawrence, Massachusetts, a strike that will capture the attention of the entire country and beyond. Protected by decades of tariffs in the latter part of the nineteenth century, Lawrence's mill owners have become fabulously wealthy. Despite owning mansions up and down the East Coast, as well as yachts and too many automobiles to count, they continued to argue that they couldn't afford to pay workers enough to keep them out of grinding poverty. The owners believed, in essence, that the money was theirs. Was it not their capital investments that built the enormous mills that housed the new power looms that were the envy of the industrialized world and which drew workers from all over the planet? For their part, the workers' demands were not unreasonable, but underlying them was a deeply held conviction that made owners uncomfortable—that the dinero, or a larger share of it, was rightfully theirs by virtue of the fact that they, not the owners, produced it. If such a principle were ever granted, where would such demands end? Here is the root quarrel that is always exacerbated in times of disruption, and it's Mr. E. H. Harriman's justification for shelling out all that money to outfit that posse to deal with a bunch of two-bit outlaws. John Huston's character, Noah Cross, famously explains the whole deal to Jake Gittes in *Chinatown*. After Cross admits he has no idea how much he's worth, Gittes asks the question working stiffs always ask: What's all that money *for*? Cross answers without hesitation, "The future, Mr. Gittes. The future."

The Future

The richest of the Lawrence mill owners was William Wood, whose parents were poor Portuguese immigrants. Their last name was actually Silva, which translates into English as "wood." Only twelve years old when his father died, young William dropped out of school to provide for his mother and younger siblings. Driven to succeed, he became one of the richest men in New England, and he seemed to believe that his success could be replicated by anyone willing to work as hard as he did, a conviction shared by many wealthy men of the period who had a similar acquaintance with childhood poverty. Indeed, Wood's staggering success may actually have been justification for sharing so little of his wealth with the men and women who worked at his mills. The way he apparently saw it, those mills were providing a valuable opportunity for the right sort of man—one capable of overcoming brutal hardship. Making such a man's life easier, Wood reasoned, did him no favors. A living wage that lifted him out of the slums and filled his belly would actually disincentivize him, encourage him to settle for less than he was capable of. Extreme hardship was where true character was forged. Hunger? Grinding poverty? Now *these* were incentives.

If such a rationale seems like a convenient excuse for hoarding wealth, we should remember that such thinking had deep roots in Puritan New England, where Calvinists believed not only in an "elect" and a "damned" but that wealth was a sign of God's approval. It's also interesting to note that with the exception of J. P. Morgan, the other famous robber barons (Carnegie, Rockefeller, Gould, Vanderbilt) all had humble beginnings, which suggests that their desire for wealth might be evidence of deep-seated and probably unacknowledged fear. Having been poor when they were young, they were determined that no one in their families would ever be poor again. How much money would be required? Well, just how poor had you been? How frightened? What's most important, any decent therapist would say, is to understand what all this striving is really about. Noah Cross hit the nail on the head. It's about the future, Mr. Gittes. The future.

Danny DeVito was also right: "Everybody needs money." Butch and Sundance certainly do throughout the film, but the way they pursue it suggests that money is not an end in itself. The way Sundance explains their always being broke to Etta is that Butch is a "soft touch" who's always loaning people money and buying drinks. *Foolish* would be one way to describe such behavior. *Generous* would be another. Though Butch and Sundance spend their whole lives pursuing money, neither appears to have any desire to be rich. When they rob the *Flyer* and the take is disappointing, Butch isn't particularly chagrined. "Just so long as we come out ahead," he says. Indeed, their easy-come, easy-go attitude toward money kind of makes you wonder what their childhoods were like. The movie offers few clues, but to me they bear a closer resemblance to frat boys who have somehow managed to get disowned by wealthy parents than to guys whose young lives were scarred by poverty.

By contrast, the son of a clergyman in upstate New York, the real-life E. H. Harriman quit school at the age of fourteen to become an errand boy on Wall Street, which begs an obvious question: Was it the atmosphere of wealth in the making there that drove him to pursue riches, or was he fleeing the austerity of his clergyman father? Hard to know, but this much is clear: whatever was driving him made him neither foolish nor generous with money. At the time of his death his estimated worth was between $150 and $200 million, all of which he left to his wife, and it took care of future Harrimans quite nicely (including William Averell Harriman, who became governor of New York, as well as ambassador to both Britain and the Soviet Union). The descendants of the Rockefellers and the Carnegies and the Vanderbilts, as we know, also fared well. In time, these families became almost as famous for their public generosity as they'd earlier been for their ruthless business practices, but of course that was long after they'd secured their families' future.

Driven

In "We Can't Make It Here" James McMurtry, angry with the men who sent the jobs away, claims, "They've never known want, they'll never know need." Similarly, Butch Cassidy, furious with E. H. Harriman for spending all that money on his elite posse, gripes, "I bet he inherited every penny he's got." This view of wealth—that greed and privilege always beget more greed and privilege, that families with generational wealth have a vested interest in keeping poor people poor—is particularly satisfying in polarized times like these. But doesn't it ignore the complicity of two other groups of people—(1) those who are not wealthy but aspire to be and plan to act like capitalists when their ship comes in, and (2) those who are *not* driven by the pursuit of wealth (and may even view capitalism with suspicion), but still "need money"? Don't things actually become more interesting and nuanced if we consider the possibility that the relentless pursuit of wealth is as likely to be rooted in the fear of poverty as in inherited wealth and privilege? Wouldn't that go a long way toward explaining the behavior not just of people like E. H. Harriman but also people like, well, me?

Because unlike Jake Gittes, I understand driven men like Harriman and Noah Cross. Indeed, many people would describe *me* as driven, and because I've made a good living as a writer, they could be forgiven for concluding that making money was what I set out to do. They'd be wrong, but they're owed an explanation, I think. Anyway, for what it's worth, I have one. Like my father, I'm stubborn beyond belief and pretty good at putting one foot in front of the other, at continuing to move forward when others, discouraged by failure, might be tempted to quit. And like my mother, I'm an optimist, though my own brand of optimism is more cautious than hers and, I'd like to think, less reliant on magical thinking when it comes to execution. But most of us who choose careers in the arts know all too well that we're unlikely to strike it rich. Indeed, the word *career*, when applied to the arts, is pretty misleading. Instead of choosing, we seem to be chosen or "called." In place of careers we have vocations. We're no less driven than your average industrialist, just more poorly paid for the long hours we both put in. Most artists require day jobs to support their habit. That's not to say there's no money to be made if you're a writer or a painter or an actor. Obviously, there is, but wealth isn't what motivates us. The fact that most artists would do what we do for free explains why so many of us do just that.

Here's the thing, though. The fact that we're not motivated by money doesn't mean that we don't think about it all the time. Artists have no more desire to be poor than anybody else. *Everybody* needs money, not everybody but artists. It's *because* we have more reason to fear poverty than most that we worry about it incessantly, which can make even people like me, who have been better paid for our efforts than we imagined we would be, less generous than we'd like to be. And even if we're not pursuing wealth, that doesn't mean we're immune to anxiety about the future. We too want to protect our loved ones and wonder how much money that will take. We may personally identify with the world's laborers—its strikers and essential pandemic workers, and even its two-bit outlaws—but we share the same impulses that cause the E. H. Harrimans of the world to withhold generosity until the future of their loved ones is safe and secure. Precisely because we *have* known want and *have* known need, we're inclined to be cautious, to doubt our skill, our talent, our agency. We're all too aware that the same mechanism that turns a spigot on also turns it off. And often ours is not the hand on the mechanism. We want to be generous and sometimes succeed, but we fear the next disruption, the one that will render our particular skills obsolete or redundant. We fear becoming Butch and Sundance, facing something we can neither imagine nor outrun.

We fear the future, Mr. Gittes. The future.

Words and Their Arrangement

Is it possible for a writer to be careless with language, or just not terribly interested in words, and still be a successful storyteller? Absolutely. In fact, I'd argue the majority of commercially successful writers are less than meticulous in their use of language, perhaps because they believe such "fine-tuning" is what editors and copy editors are for, or maybe because they're more concerned with other elements of storytelling. Genre writing in particular—romance, sci-fi, detective, horror, historical, thriller, etc.—comes with its own set of rules and expectations, and those who toil in these fields often place more of a premium on plot and narrative pacing than beautiful sentence-to-sentence writing. Of course, writers who transcend their genres—Jane Austen, Ursula Le Guin, Stephen King, Walter Mosley, Dennis Lehane—are often superb stylists who care as much about language as more "literary" writers, though they're more likely to be wary (and they're right to be) of language that calls attention to itself (*Wow! Just look at me write!*) or whose beauty is intended to distract readers from their story's lack of dramatic momentum. To be frank, literary writers are far more likely to polish a turd than their often less-pretentious genre brethren. Having said that, though, allow me to sound pretentious for a moment and assert my conviction that while it's possible to be careless with language and be a *successful* writer, it's not possible to be a *great* one, for the simple reason that words matter.

One of my own early writing teachers used to argue that the best way for aspiring writers to learn the power of words is to study simple stories that are told without much in the way of stylistic artifice. Such advice can appear counterintuitive, since it's often the great stylists—the ones with powerful, idiosyncratic voices—who attract aspiring writers to literature in the first place. Nor are they wrong to put writers like Faulkner and Joyce on pedestals. Unfortunately, their verbal gymnastics can obscure or even belie how much power can be achieved in the absence of such stylistic flourishes. To illustrate, let's look at the lyrics to "Pancho and Lefty," by the great Townes Van Zandt. It's the story of Pancho Villa and his friend Lefty, who, the song implies, betrayed him to the federales. The two opening stanzas introduce us to Pancho:

> *Living on the road, my friend*
> *Was gonna keep you free and clean*
> *Now you wear your skin like iron*
> *And your breath's as hard as kerosene*
> *Your weren't your mama's only boy*
> *But her favorite one, it seems*
> *She began to cry when you said goodbye*
> *And sank into your dreams.*
>
> *Pancho was a bandit, boys*
> *His horse was fast as polished steel*
> *Wore his gun outside his pants*

For all the honest world to feel
But Pancho met his match, you know
On the deserts down in Mexico
And nobody heard his dying words
Ah, but that's the way it goes.

Notice that in the first stanza Pancho is referred to as "you" and "my friend." Is the speaker Van Zandt himself? Lefty? It's impossible to know for certain, but whoever is speaking appears to be on intimate terms, someone who knows not only Pancho and what he has done but also why. Living on the road was supposed to keep him "free and clean," but the result has been the exact opposite. No longer the boy who left his grieving mother, Pancho has learned to wear his skin "like iron," and his breath is "hard as kerosene." Once on his own, we're informed, he "sank into" his dreams. *Sank* is a surprising word choice. Normally we would *slip* or maybe *slide* or *drift* into a dream, all words that suggest how gentle, graceful and pleasurable the process can be. They also sound voluntary. By contrast, Pancho's sinking feels more violent and implies a loss of control. It's not like he woke up one morning and decided that maybe law school wasn't for him. His decision to become an outlaw, once made, is irreversible.

It's worth noting that though the task of introducing Pancho remains the same in the second stanza, its implied audience has changed. Gone now are both the *you* and *my friend* of the first stanza, replaced here with *boys*. So who are they? A group of journalists? Historians? All we can say for sure is that they've already heard of Pancho (who "met his match, *you know* / On the deserts down in Mexico"). They already know the broad strokes of his story, which means that whoever is speaking to them (again, maybe Lefty?) is offering insider—perhaps even eyewitness—information. He tells them that Pancho's horse "was fast as polished steel," and that he wore his gun "outside his pants / For all the honest world to feel." *Outside his pants* (as opposed to, say, *holstered*) is an unusual phrase that calls attention to Pancho's lack of interest in concealment; he's an open-carry kind of guy. But it's the second part of the sentence—*for all the honest world to feel*—that contains the real surprise. Given what the sentence is about (Pancho's refusal to conceal his gun), we expect the final word to be *see*. *Feel* momentarily wrong-foots us, and we go looking for an explanation. Noticing that *see* doesn't rhyme with *steel*, we conclude that Van Zandt must've really wanted the rhyme, because, given the choice, he opted for sound over sense. It's possible.

On the other hand, what if *feel* really is the word Van Zandt both wanted and meant? What's the difference between *seeing* Pancho's gun and *feeling* it? What if the whole point is for people to *feel* the gun he carries, its potential to maim or even kill? What if it's the gun that allows people to notice Pancho himself, which they might not otherwise do? What if it's the gun that makes him somebody? What if his need to *be* somebody important is the dream he sank into? If so, then you have to wonder: Did Van Zandt choose the word *feel* because it rhymes with *steel*? Or did he choose *steel* so that he could later deploy *feel* at the end of the line? To me, this second explanation makes more sense because the resulting meaning is richer, less literal. It also squares better with my experience of telling stories. People who aren't storytellers are inclined to believe that the words sit on the page in the order that they first occurred to the writer. If Van Zandt thought of the word *steel* first, then he must've been looking for a word to rhyme with it (and *feel* does). But this assumes that writers don't revise, and of course they do. The sequence of words in the first draft may have little to do with their arrangement in the final draft, which might be written a month or even a year later. Each draft clarifies not only which words are the right ones but also that they've been arranged in the best possible order for optimal effect. The word *feel* might be the last word in the stanza, but Van Zandt may have become convinced of its importance early on. For all we know, he constructed the entire stanza with that word in mind. To the uninitiated, that might seem like starting out with a radiator cap and installing a whole car around it, but sometimes that's the way art works.

Only after Pancho has "met his match" in the desert, halfway through the song, do we meet Lefty (unless it's his voice we've been listening to all along, to me an attractive interpretation).

> *And Lefty, he can't sing the blues*
> *All night long like he used to*
> *The dust that Pancho bit down south*
> *Ended up in Lefty's mouth*
> *The day they laid poor Pancho low*
> *Lefty split for Ohio*
> *Where he got the bread to go*
> *Oh, there ain't nobody knows.*

"The dust that Pancho bit down south" is, for my money, the best wordplay in the song. We're all familiar with "bite the dust" as a figure of speech, but here Van Zandt turns the cliché on its head by altering the syntax. The phrasing we would expect is "Pancho bit the dust down south"—the subject of the sentence being *Pancho*, and *dust* its direct object. By making *dust* the subject and locating "Pancho bit" in a subordinate structure, we're again wrong-footed, this time in a truly wonderful way. Now "bite the dust" isn't so recognizable as a cliché, and the sentence's new subject *dust* becomes more shocking by ending up in Lefty's mouth. Lefty not only hasn't forgotten Pancho, his old friend has become the centerpiece of Lefty's own, equally tragic life. We're urged not to judge Lefty too harshly, because "he only did what he had to do." But apparently Lefty himself doesn't agree. He's not only kept Pancho alive but amplified his own betrayal, thereby increasing his guilt and suffering. Pancho's sins were punishable by death; Lefty's, ironically, by a long life.

There's plenty of word magic in the song's chorus, too:

> *And all the federales say*
> *They could've had him any day*
> *They only let him hang around*
> *Out of kindness, I suppose.*

The first time you hear the song, you may well miss the subtle changes in the third line. True, the chorus contains the same insistence each time it repeats: that the federales could have dispensed with Pancho at any point. The second time through, however, *hang around* becomes *slip away*. The third time through they admit to letting him *go so wrong*. The pattern that emerges may be subtle, but it's also significant. *Hang around* and *slip away* both suggest that Pancho was merely an annoyance. But when the federales admit they let him *go so wrong*, they're acknowledging not only that he was always more than an annoyance, but also their complicity in what ultimately happened to him. It's also worth noting that if the way we see Pancho changes each time the chorus repeats, the same is true of the federales themselves. The first time through we're told what *all the federales say*. If they all say the same thing, it must be true, right? Except that the claim begs an obvious question. If they could've put an end to his banditry earlier, why on earth didn't they? The motive we're asked to entertain could not be more ridiculous: they've let Pancho go "out of kindness, *I suppose*." Each time the chorus repeats, the claim becomes more ludicrous, especially the final time, when Van Zandt alters it slightly. Now, instead of *all the federales say*, it's *a few gray federales say*, and the new message is clear: lies become more transparent over time. The first draft of history may be written by the victors, but first drafts exist—like poems and songs—to be revised, as many times as it takes, until the story makes sense, until it squares with our experience of how the world works. In the end Van Zandt seems less interested in Pancho and Lefty themselves than that we understand how history operates, that we should be skeptical of both its facts and its lessons. The phrase that's left ringing in our ears is that final "I suppose." How marvelously cagey those two words are, the way they force us to revisit everything "we're told" to arrive at the truth. "Ain't nobody knows" where Lefty got the money to go to Ohio actually means that *everybody* does. In truth, *nobody* supposes that the federales were motivated by kindness. And only a damned fool believes what he's told when the facts don't add up.

Okay, but why spend so much time analyzing such a simple, seemingly straightforward song? Well, for one thing, to demonstrate that a good story's best trick is to make the telling look easy, natural and inevitable, as if anybody could do it. But that's after-the-fact, federale logic. If they could've had Pancho any day, they would've. And not everybody *could* pull off what Van Zandt does in "Pancho and Lefty"; if they could, they would. Even more important is that aspiring writers too often worry about all the wrong things. Is their vocabulary sufficient to their ambitions? Are they sophisticated enough?

Is the language flashy enough to get noticed by agents or editors? (Should you, like Pancho, wear your gun outside your pants?) A song like "Pancho and Lefty" is important to study precisely because Van Zandt is worried about the right things. There isn't an ounce of self-consciousness anywhere. His diction couldn't be less pretentious: only two words in the entire song—*federales* and *kerosene*—contain more than two syllables. Great art, it seems, can be made of humble materials.

Good to know.

From *Lucky Jim* to *Lucky Hank*

When I started writing *Straight Man*, the novel that spawned AMC's hit series *Lucky Hank*, I thought I was writing an academic satire like *Lucky Jim*, which I'd read as a grad student, long before I dreamed of becoming a writer myself. I'd been storing up tales of academic lunacy since I began teaching back in the 1970s, and it all came gushing out as soon as I put pen to paper, a burst dam of hilarious, often-outrageous material, a gift that kept on giving. My earlier novels all had to be teased out and coaxed into being, a process not unlike childbirth (I'm told) in that the labor is intense enough to produce amnesia, its difficulty, once overcome, no longer worth remembering, its time line irrelevant. How was *The Risk Pool* conceived? Who cares? Like your newborn child, it's sweet and healthy and you love it and that's all that matters.

Perhaps because birthing *Straight Man* wasn't so "labor intensive," I'm able to remember exactly where and when it was conceived. My first full-time academic gig was at a branch campus of Penn State in Altoona, and one late-August afternoon I went for a stroll around the duck pond with the dean of faculty. It was a week or two before the start of fall classes, and he still didn't have his budget, which meant he couldn't hire additional part-time faculty to cover the sections of freshman comp not being taught by "regular" faculty like me. Every year it was the same, he complained, the legislature in Harrisburg holding the money hostage until the last moment, causing the adjunct faculty unnecessary anxiety and frustration, which they took out on him, despite his having exactly no leverage in the matter. "What am I supposed to do?" he sighed, pausing to examine the bottom of his shoe for duck guano. "Threaten to kill a duck a day until they give me the money?"

Okay, that was when the book was conceived, but it was another full decade before William Henry Devereaux Jr., chair of the English Department at West Central Pennsylvania State University in fictional Railton, would make this very threat in my novel, and it would be decades longer before Bob Odenkirk would offer a much-watered-down version of that threat (to box a goose a day until he gets *his* budget) in *Lucky Hank*. (The novel's title had to be changed because the term *straight man* no longer meant what it did back when imaginary ducks could still be threatened, provided no actual ducks were harmed during filming.)

As I said, I began the book thinking it would be an academic satire, but as the manuscript pages piled up, I began to suspect that the book's real subject was middle age, in particular that odd sense of loss that can derive from financial security. If true, that put the book at odds with *Lucky Jim* and most other academic satires where the plot hinges on financial *in*security. Untenured and vulnerable, the protagonists of true academic satires, like Jim Dixon, fear losing their jobs and having no future. I had to wonder: Was it even possible to write an interesting academic novel about characters who have been granted tenure and promotion and therefore *can't* be fired? Don't all good books depend on putting characters in jeopardy and thereby raising the dramatic stakes? For a novel like the one I was writing to work, tenure and promotion would have to trail some other danger as real as the fear of losing one's livelihood, and that's a much-more-challenging task than making fun of academics, who, after all, tee the ball up and practically beg you to whack it.

The solution, of course, was to make tenure metaphorical. Middle age offers many different kinds of tenure. In addition to your job, you can also be tenured in your marriage, your friendships and even in your material possessions. Such security comes at a price, of course. Marriage, children, friends and mortgages can root you to the spot, prevent you from pulling up stakes should a thrilling new opportunity arise. Securely tethered, you begin to miss your younger self. *That* lucky bastard got to choose which doors to open and walk through. And what a bloody fool he was! Excited by his agency, he barely noticed when those doors closed and locked behind him. Middle age, it turns out, is all about living with the consequences of choices your younger self was only vaguely aware of making at the time. It's only in their aftermath that you remember old girlfriends, other job offers you turned down, that great place your parents took you to when you were a kid and where you imagined you might end up living. And what about all the other important things you meant to do? There were, you now recall, lots of these, and now you'll never be able to do any of them, not without doing harm to others and possibly yourself. Sure, you love your wife, your friends, your kids, maybe even your job, but you still can't help feeling cheated, even if the person who cheated you is you. *Especially* if that person is you. Perhaps most of all, you regret the loss of the very insecurity you strove to remove. "What I expected," Stephen Spender writes in one of his most famous poems, "was . . . fighting, . . . struggles, . . . and climbing." By contrast, tenure offers those fortunate enough to secure it "the gradual day, weakening the will, leaking the brightness away."

Nor is it just academics who are bedeviled by what trails in the wake of security. As *Straight Man* begins, Hank is sitting with his friend Teddy Barnes at a railroad crossing where earlier in the week a Conrail worker named William Cherry, having retired with full benefits, lay down on the tracks in the middle of the night and was decapitated by a passing train. Though William Cherry's and Hank's lived experience couldn't have been much more different, Hank sympathizes. Indeed, throughout the novel his thoughts return to Cherry so frequently that the reader can't help wondering if Hank himself has a death wish.

Academic satires, then, are usually propelled by the fear that things won't work out. Apparently, I was writing a novel that posed, at least for a man like Hank, the equally terrifying possibility that things will. Indeed, they already have, and there isn't a damn thing to be done about it.

AT THE TIME I was writing *Straight Man* my own circumstance was not entirely unlike Hank's. I was teaching at Colby College, where I'd recently been granted tenure and promoted to full professor, though I'd asked for neither and actually declined to fill out the requisite paperwork. In fact, I shared a full-time position with another writer, and part-timers generally weren't awarded tenure. How could I have been so blasé about a promotion that would mean more money and status and job security? Well, an earlier novel of mine, *Nobody's Fool*, had been purchased by Paramount and would start filming soon, and my fondest hope was that the movie would be a hit and allow me to become a full-time writer. By tenuring and promoting me, the college was offering me the kind of cushy academic life that would tempt me to continue teaching. My daughters were still young, and I had several other family financial obligations, which meant that, much as I might want to, I couldn't just quit my job, at least not yet. What I *could* do, though, was work to undermine, even destabilize, the security I was being offered. By writing an academic satire, by making fun of academics and the academy itself, I could prevent the life I didn't want and feared I might be stuck with. *Straight Man* would make me persona non grata on every college campus in America and leave me no choice but to become the full-time writer I wanted to be. Maybe I couldn't afford to quit my job *now*, but I could kick the can down the road. The book would take two years to finish and another year for it to come out and piss everybody off. I had three years to make this work. The clock was ticking.

The crazy thing is that this act of self-sabotage actually worked, though not in the way I imagined. When the novel came out, it not only didn't get me ostracized from the academy as I'd hoped, it actually resulted in a deluge of speaking engagements. Even at the universities where I'd taught before coming to Colby, my former colleagues, whom I'd expected to recognize themselves and hold grudges, identified only their colleagues. Newly elected department chairs and deans were gifted be-careful-what-you-wish-for copies of the novel. I even gave the commencement address at Altoona, where the onstage faculty wore the plastic nose and glasses that Hank Devereaux wears when threatening to kill ducks. I felt a little like the Zero Mostel character in *The Producers* who asks, "Where did I go right?"

The book was also well received by critics, but it was the wife of one of my English department colleagues at Colby who said what pleased me most. "I expected the book to be funny," she told me, a puzzled expression on her face, "but I didn't expect to be so moved." Which meant I'd been right. Though *Straight Man* owes an enormous debt to *Lucky Jim*, its objective, in the end, wasn't satire. Amis's novel contains some of the funniest and most memorable set pieces I've ever read, but because it's a real satire and not, like *Straight Man,* just masquerading as one, it's simply impossible to imagine a reader being moved by it. Both novels enjoy mocking human behavior and institutions, but *Lucky Jim*'s derision is fully sufficient and satisfying to its author's purposes. Reading the novel, you can't help but feel and share Amis's delight in his task. You can almost hear him chortling at the sheer wickedness of his wit. He never doubts that the characters and behaviors he's skewering deserve it. He feels not the slightest sympathy for Professor Welch or his wife or their son, Bertrand, the novel's principal satirical targets, and it's great fun watching them get the comeuppance they so richly deserve, even more fun, at least to my mind, than watching Jim Dixon, the novel's protagonist, come out on top, probably because he so clearly *doesn't* deserve to. By the end of the novel, Dixon does discover and assert something like agency by jettisoning his usual subservience and making fun of everything the Welches stand for, but his doing so is undermined by the fact that he's blind drunk at the time. Sober, Amis implies, he never would have found the necessary courage. Moreover, his behavior throughout the novel appears completely untethered from anything like morality. He simply identifies whatever he must do to keep the job he hates and then does it, even if it means groveling and a steady diet of humiliation. He's chosen medieval history as his field of study not out of any particular interest but rather as the path of least resistance. Indeed, at the end of the book, Dixon seems even more profoundly cynical than he was at the beginning, concluding that manipulative Margaret Peel's miserable life is simply the result of her being physically unattractive, just as Christine's Callaghan's good fortune is preordained by the fact that she's sexy. This may be unfair, but the way Dixon sees it, there isn't much point in worrying about it. His own unexpected success he attributes, correctly, to dumb luck. True, we readers prefer him and Christine to the Welches because they're at least honest with themselves, but the difference is one of degree, and that's the thing about satire: it can come off as mean-spirited because the writer has assumed a perch that allows him to view the world and its inhabitants from a distance and never participates in their folly. Satire doesn't urge us to feel sympathy but rather to judge. Once sympathy—which can turn into love if you aren't careful—enters the picture, everything changes and becomes more complicated.

TURNING A THIRTY-YEAR-OLD NOVEL like *Straight Man* into a TV show like *Lucky Hank* isn't easy. A lot has changed. But it would be a difficult task even without the time lapse. The producers of *Election,* Tom Perrotta's comic novel of the same name, secured the rights to the book when it was still in manuscript, and the movie started filming before the book came out. Even so, Alexander Payne, its writer-director, had to ask himself some fundamental questions: What kind of movie am I making here? How should the story be told? Because what works in a novel doesn't always work on-screen. What Payne decided to make was a satire, and it's not difficult to understand why. Like *Straight Man,* Perrotta's novel contained numerous satirical elements. National politics, it slyly suggested, isn't so different from high school; indeed, they may be a natural outgrowth of adolescent behavior. This unexpected analogy could be lifted straight from the book. The problem was that while Perrotta was clearly poking fun, he'd also invested considerable sympathy for the plight of his characters, and in a satire much of that sympathy would have to be stripped away. Tracy Flick, in particular, would have to go from being a bright, ambitious student who's being raised by a single mom and who deserves, by virtue of her intelligence and work ethic, to be elected student body president, to a genuine monster of ambition, whose dishonest, cutthroat tactics will not only ensure her victory in the high-school election but also propel her, later in life, into the highest echelons of government. Then there's the question of how to tell the story. Perrotta's novel is ensemble in nature, and its most important characters all get their moment or moments in the spotlight. If Tracy Flick is going to step forward in the film version, others will have to step back, their sympathy reined in, lest we *feel* for them when we're supposed to be *thinking* about how they reveal the way national politics exhibits all the essential features of high-school drama.

If it seems like I'm taking sides here, preferring the novel to the movie, I'm not. I actually happen to love both iterations. I'm simply pointing out that novelists who are lucky enough to have their work adapted for the screen cannot expect screenwriters to share their own particular vision, much less the personal obsessions from which those visions flow. Nor is it a competition. Decades after Perrotta's novel was made into a movie, he wrote the sequel *Tracy Flick Can't Win,* which also contains sly, satirical elements. But Perrotta, in control of the narrative again, doubles down on his original intention by creating a new ensemble cast of characters and investing them with considerable sympathy, even as he shrewdly diagnoses what ails them. He's not arguing with the movie Alexander Payne made of his novel but rather is in conversation with it. He's well aware that this sequel could also find its way to the screen, with Payne (and Reese Witherspoon) again at the helm.

AS EXECUTIVE PRODUCER of *Lucky Hank,* I had the opportunity to read and comment on its first season's scripts, and I was delighted to discover in these that the show's writers understood that *Straight Man* both was and was not a traditional academic satire, that the show's characters, some of whom were not even in the novel, would be invested with sympathy and understanding no matter how foolishly they behaved. The English department in *Lucky Hank* is considerably younger than the one in *Straight Man,* but Hank and his wife, Lily, the two central characters, are tenured like Hank and Lily are in the novel: by their jobs, yes, but also in their marriage and by parenthood and real estate. As a result, they have too much security, not too little. As in the novel, their brightness is leaking away. We sympathize, and so, apparently, did *Lucky Hank'*s showrunners, Paul Lieberstein and Aaron Zelman, though this is hardly surprising, given that both worked on the American version of *The Office* when it was winning Emmys left and right. Getting viewers to sympathize with deeply flawed, often-foolhardy characters was hardly a new challenge. Still, they had to have asked themselves the same question Alexander Payne did: What sort of show would *Lucky Hank* be? A comedy? A dramedy? Which of the novel's elements would be highlighted? Which would recede into the background?

For instance, what role would setting play? All stories are set somewhere, but all settings are not equally important. *Lucky Jim,* for instance, is set somewhere in the English Midlands, but Kingsley Amis makes a point of keeping descriptions to a minimum. What's important is that it *isn't* set in Cambridge or Oxford, where the ancient buildings are made of stone. In Amis's provincial university the buildings are all made of red brick, the implication being that they aren't worth describing in detail because nothing of real importance happens in them.

Setting-wise, American television comedies tend to fall into two camps. In the first, setting is clearly established in the opening credits, then mostly forgotten. *The Office,* for instance, is set in Scranton, Pennsylvania, and the show's writers clearly did their homework, getting details about the city right. Similarly, as established in its opening credits, the old *Mary Tyler Moore Show* takes place in Minneapolis. What these shows seem to suggest is that an office is an office, and a newsroom is a newsroom. Practically speaking, after the credits, you're going to be indoors. The interiors are what will matter; the shows themselves can be shot anywhere. By contrast, *Seinfeld* isn't just set in New York; its characters are creatures of that city and no other. Jerry, George, Elaine and Kramer are inseparable from it, as are, decades later, the characters in *Fleishman Is in Trouble,* and in both shows exteriors are made use of well beyond the opening credits. Cities, such shows imply, are not interchangeable, like offices or newsrooms. They leave a mark on the people who live in them.

Or take class, which plays a role in most of my novels, including *Straight Man.* Class also figures prominently in *Lucky Jim,* whose plot is driven by the influx of veterans who flooded provincial universities after the Second World War. Many were middle- or lower-middle-class guys who lacked not only the proper Oxbridge educations of their senior professors but also their genteel manners. It was painfully clear that they would not fit in, or be allowed to, until people like the Welches retired. In *Straight Man* the real class divide is between town and gown.

Railton's principal employer is Conrail, and the city's poor live close to the tracks, where everything is coated with layers of smoke and grime, whereas the campus itself is located on the city's outskirts, where the air is cleaner. Its faculty can afford to live farther from the rail yard, either in the healthier suburbs or higher up in the mountains, where the dirty city below is out of both sight and mind. One of the problems facing the creators of *Lucky Hank* is that class struggle is more often the subject of dramas than comedies. It plays a relatively minor role in *The Office*, though it occasionally surfaces between the Dunder Mifflin employees who work in the office and those who toil in the warehouse. *Seinfeld* doesn't have a lot to say about class, probably because the show is really less about New York City as a whole than one of its many neighborhoods, the Upper West Side, which, like neighborhoods in most big cities, self-selects along racial and economic lines. At any rate, the fact that class may be a particular obsession of mine doesn't mean that it can or should be shoehorned into *Lucky Hank*, whose writers will have their own obsessions, ones that also derive from their own lived experience. In 2023, the show will need to deal with other issues, like representation, that weren't on my radar in 1997. Readers of the novel will notice immediately that *Lucky Hank*'s English department is far more diverse than mine in the book. Back when I was teaching at Penn State Altoona, long before I wrote *Straight Man*, I recall only one Black faculty member across all academic disciplines. That's changed across higher education and maybe, for all I know, even in central Pennsylvania, which James Carville once famously described as Alabama. To some viewers *Lucky Hank*'s English department may be evidence of "wokeness," of networks demanding that boxes be ticked in order to satisfy new diversity initiatives. Actually, though, the problem has been around for a while. I'm old enough to remember cop shows in the seventies where urban street gangs were racially diverse. No such thing ever happened in real life, but the writers were no doubt reluctant to imply that crime in America had an exclusively black or brown face. *Lucky Hank*'s writers face a similar dilemma. Which truth do you emphasize? That university faculties in general are far more diverse than they were thirty years ago? Or that the very last institutions to diversify, for all kinds of reasons, are those like West Central Pennsylvania State University in Railton?

Also germane to any TV show with an academic setting is the question of education itself. How much of *Lucky Hank* will take place in the classroom? How will student-teacher conferences factor in? How will adjunct instructors be treated? What will students want from the teachers? What will Hank and his colleagues expect from their students? How will the student-teacher relationship differ from Devereaux Sr.'s relationship to his students at Columbia? (Hint: a lot.) *Straight Man* focused on the mismatch of the university's students to its faculty. Many of the former are the first in their families to attend college, and their uneducated parents see education as job training. Their professors, not surprisingly, see things differently. Helping students get well-paying jobs isn't their primary mandate. In the novel, most of Hank's colleagues not only have degrees from elite universities like Columbia, but once had dreams of teaching in such institutions themselves, of having stellar careers like Hank's father. Now they know they never will, and that knowledge has left them bitter. In my considerable experience of teaching in large, underfunded state universities, this student-faculty mismatch was pretty common. My students in second-tier state universities like SIU Carbondale and Southern Connecticut State were as bright and talented as those I taught at Colby, an expensive, elite liberal arts college, but, like the postwar generation of students and teachers in *Lucky Jim*, they hadn't quite figured out how to *be* college students yet. When it came to choosing majors, they were driven by practical considerations. They couldn't *afford* to study English or art or philosophy beyond the school's basic humanities requirements. Even if they wanted to major in art, their parents wouldn't have stood for it.

They were also, despite their native intelligence, more likely to be naïve and emotionally immature. Before coming to the university, they'd seen very little of the world. The homes they grew up in were not full of books. In *Straight Man*, Hank's workshop students, Leo and Solange, are good examples. He's writing misogynistic slasher tales, she ethereal language-infused stories featuring clouds. Hank doesn't see either of them as ungifted or as a waste of his time. He just suspects they both desperately need to get laid. He's certain that this simple, Occam's razor–like solution to a complex problem would greatly improve their academic performance. Teaching at Colby College, I learned that students from wealthy families also had challenging problems, but unlike my students at large, underfunded public universities, students at expensive private colleges never doubted they belonged. They had grown up in homes that were full of books and pianos, and they'd gone on vacations to faraway places. If they were troubled by self-doubt, they disguised it well.

My point here is that *Lucky Hank*'s writers may have spent more time as students in elite institutions like Colby than SIU Carbondale (where, interestingly, Bob Odenkirk was an undergraduate). If so, they may not have concluded, as I have, that the future of our democracy does not depend on the success of our own Oxbridge institutions, like Amherst and Yale, but rather on the nation's public universities and even its community colleges. (What good is it to be Ivy League educated if you end up Ted Cruz or Ron DeSantis?) *Lucky Hank*'s writers may share my admittedly radical views, but then again, they may not. In either case the educational world they create will derive from their own lived experience, not mine, not Kingsley Amis's. Inevitably, they will chart their own course.

It's worth remembering, too, that some important decisions about the content of *Lucky Hank* may not be determined by its writers. The fact that a story is set somewhere doesn't mean it will be shot there. The miniseries made of my novel *Empire Falls* was shot in Maine, where the story was set, but several other locations were scouted, including Massachusetts, which offered financial incentives (Maine did not) and Canada, where everything can be done more inexpensively. When the HBO location scouts finally agreed to give Maine a look, they were bowled over. "Wow!" they said, after stops in Waterville, Winslow and Skowhegan. "This is perfect!" (Duh. These were the places I was describing when I wrote the book.) And having seen how perfect it was, HBO decided to spend the money. But that, remember, was a two-part limited miniseries and a drama. Long-running comedies and dramedies are seldom given such generous budgets, which was why I wasn't surprised to learn that *Lucky Hank* would be shot in Vancouver, not central Pennsylvania. I have little doubt that if AMC's location scouts visited Altoona their reaction would have been the same as those HBO scouts who reluctantly came to Maine. The campus itself, the duck pond, downtown Altoona with its huge dirty rail yard, the outlying communities where the story's faculty reside—all of it would've been perfect. But *Lucky Hank* was a comedy designed to run several seasons, and most of it would be shot indoors. A classroom is a classroom, an English department an English department.

. . .

WHAT A TV SHOW's writers *do* have control over is style. The central storytelling conceit of *The Office* was that Michael Scott and the other employees at Dunder Mifflin were being interviewed on camera as events unfolded in real time. In effect, this means that there are two cameras at work at all times. There's the usual implied camera that's shooting a show called *The Office* and also the one that's part of the story, recording those interviews. Lest we forget its existence, Michael, Jim, Pam and the others will nervously glance in its direction, as if to ask whoever is holding it, *Did you catch that? Straight Man's* storytelling—a simple, straightforward first-person narrative—couldn't be more different. I usually avoid first-person point of view in my novels because the only truly compelling reason for using it, I believe, is that both the voice of the narrator and his way of looking at the world are idiosyncratic and central to the story's telling. For me, the principal pleasure of reading *Straight Man* is dwelling in Hank Devereaux's head, and thereby escaping my own very different one. Unfortunately, adapting first-person narratives for the screen can be challenging. (Third-person narrations look *at* the story's characters, not *through* them. We learn who these people are by watching them do and say things, which is exactly how film works.) If you think of a novel's first-person point of view as a camera, you immediately see the difficulty because that camera is located where no real camera could ever be situated: *inside* the main character's head, looking out from behind his eyes as he navigates the world. You could mimic that navigation by using a jerky handheld camera, turning it to the left or right to simulate which direction the character is looking, but you wouldn't be able to tell a whole story that way, and even if you could, it would still be impossible to replicate what first-person narration in a novel does so effortlessly by offering direct access to a character's thoughts. Film attempts to mitigate this problem with voice-over, which *Lucky Hank* makes use of, despite the industry's long-standing prejudice against it. The device seems to work best when what we're being told contradicts what we're seeing, thereby implying that the narrator is either lying or is naïve and doesn't understand what he's witnessing. Otherwise, viewers resent being told something they've already been shown. (If we're seeing it, the logic goes, that should be sufficient.) Using voice-over to convey information we haven't seen on the screen can be an uphill battle. In a medium designed for showing, telling has minimal impact.

Somewhat counterintuitively, what comes closest to replicating the experience of a first-person narrative on the page is the use of extreme close-ups that linger on a character's face, and this is what *Lucky Hank* does so effectively Yes, we're still looking *at* that character, but being so close, together with the fact that there's nothing else on screen to distract us, sort of invites us inside, encourages us to identify with him, to imagine what's going on in his head, to feel his joy or sorrow or pain or fear. It helps, of course, to be looking at an actor like Bob Odenkirk, whose face, especially in silence and stillness, evokes so much of Hank's inner life. You say to yourself, *I know* just *how he feels.* You don't, of course. You're guessing, and on the page, you wouldn't have to. But unlike satire, which thrives on distance and activity, good acting, like good writing, encourages empathy by getting in close and slowing things down.

IN THE RUN-UP to *Lucky Hank,* I got lots of requests for interviews, especially here in Maine, where I live. What everyone wanted to know, of course, was whether I was involved in the writing of the show, how well I thought *Lucky Hank* measured up to *Straight Man* and how "faithful" to the book the show would be. I declined all these requests, explaining that *Lucky Hank's* writers were using my novel as a launching pad for their own updated story. They, not the novel's author, deserved to be in the spotlight. Nor did I visit the set, where I would have been, at best, a distraction; at worst, seen as meddling. Instead, I communicated script notes to the series producer, who could decide whether to share them and when and in what form. Before filming started, Bob Odenkirk called with a couple specific questions about Hank, which I answered the best I could, probably not very well. Everything I knew about him was already in the book. In my experience actors are most insecure and vulnerable before filming starts, and why not? Like writers, they're pretending to be somebody they aren't. Do they know enough, understand enough, to pull that off? Paul Newman once asked me what kind of music Sully liked to listen to and was disappointed to learn that I had no more idea than he did. Actually, authors, in the flesh, often disappoint. Some years ago, on book tour, I met a fan who expressed surprise and—it seemed to me—chagrin at my height (five foot seven). "It's true," I shrugged, sharing his disappointment. "I write like a much-taller man."

What people seem to want when they talk to authors is what publishers call "added value." They've read your book; what they're curious to know is what *else* you've got. What we have to offer, alas, is often less, not more. Our best is on the page. In real life we exhibit the same flaws as other people. Oh, we try to be charming and generous, but the truth is we gave at work. Worse, there's something about having our stories adapted for the screen that causes our vanity and pettiness and territoriality to surface. We know full well that when we surrender our work to screenwriters and filmmakers and actors, their vision may differ from ours. (Count on it, in fact.) We understand that this is exactly as it should be, but guess what? It still chafes. Part of us wants to retain ownership of the thing we've surrendered (and, yes, were paid for). We've become Gollum: it's our *Precious*. Secretly, we believe that we should be writing this film, or, if we *are* writing it, that we should be directing it. Maybe even starring in it. Which is bizarre, because when we were actually writing the book, we were beset by self-doubt at every turn: *Was what I wrote today any good? Can I make it better tomorrow? Ever?* What the making of art engenders on a daily basis is humility. Once the thing is made, though, all bets are off. A switch gets flipped. Suddenly we see ourselves as victorious and the thing we made as evidence of our triumph over adversity. And what is a film, really, but a victory lap? Why should someone else get to take it?

There's nothing to do with such ugly thoughts but tamp them down, or try to. What you can't do—or at least I can't—is completely silence that little interior voice that wants to scream, *No! No! No! You're doing it all wrong.* I remember wanting to scream that at my good friend Robert Benton when he showed me his script for *Nobody's Fool*, and again at Fred Schepisi when he was shooting *Empire Falls*, and, yes, I've wanted to scream at those involved in *Lucky Hank*. *Why did you leave out the ——? Why did you change the ——? Hank would never say ——.* The corrective to such lunacy comes from just about everyone not named Richard Russo, from viewers who have read and loved the novels these films were based on. You quickly discover that *they* aren't particularly troubled by what was left out. Yeah, they did change that one detail you were really proud of, but so what? And *of course* Hank would say that. He just did. Weren't you listening? Richard Russo's real problem is that before his

novel was adapted for the screen, there was already a film running in his head, and it is this private film that the actual one
violates. There's only one solution to Richard Russo's problem:
get over it.

And I will. I promise.

Coming Clean

I have to admit, I read the new Paul Newman autobiography (*Paul Newman: The Extraordinary Life of an Ordinary Man*) with a sinking heart, partly because I suspected that what I was reading wasn't the book Newman had in mind when, over a five-year period, he and his screenwriter friend Stewart Stern recorded many hours of conversation about Paul's life. Nor, I feared, was it the book that David Rosenthal envisioned when he condensed and edited thousands of pages of transcripts (the original tapes were missing) so the autobiography, if that's what it is, could be published. Newman's purpose was and is crystal clear. He wanted to come clean about his life: his troubled childhood, his rowdy college years, his first marriage and the tragic death by overdose of his son Scott, Newman's long affair and finally marriage to Joanne Woodward, his alcoholism, his career as an actor, as well as his ongoing guilt over the fact that what so many others struggled to attain—money, fame, women, awards—came to him so easily. What he was, Newman believed, was lucky. He wanted the book to be honest about that and everything else, and he demanded that same honesty of the family members, childhood pals, old army buddies, film directors and fellow actors who provide context and offer commentary throughout the book.

Alas, Newman's insistence on fierce honesty does not always align with what appears to be the mission of his daughters, at least two of whom were involved in the publication of this book. On the one hand, the goal seems to be to dispel the fairy-tale version of their parents' marriage favored by the press, but they seem equally determined not to sully the memory of the father they loved—and, really, can you blame them? My own daughters, I suspect, would do much the same thing. For their mother's sake as much as my own, they would want no part of undermining my life's work even if, for some bizarre reason, I myself were inclined to. It could also be argued that Newman's desire to paint a warts-and-all self-portrait doesn't in and of itself guarantee a result that would be more "true" than the memory of him that his daughters hope to preserve. After all, honesty motivated by profound regret is no less prone to distortion than egotism, and I think many of the book's readers will sense, as I did, that Newman is harder on himself than God would be. (*Fine, have it your way,* I can imagine God saying. *But I hope you don't think you can bullshit* me *into believing that the man who gave the world Hud and Butch Cassidy and Cool Hand Luke, who created Newman's Own and the Hole in the Wall Gang Camps for kids, wasn't also smart, talented, driven, loyal, incredibly hardworking and concerned about his fellow man. And please don't tell me you're not a good man. I'll be the judge of that.*) More to the point, even if some of the more salacious material in the Stern transcripts has been diluted, Newman's voice comes through loud and clear, offering a first-person glimpse into the heart and mind of a man we imagined we knew. The book provides compelling evidence we didn't.

All of this said, another reason my heart sank when I read the book is more personal. Quite simply, Paul's portrayal of

Sully in Robert Benton's film of my novel *Nobody's Fool* changed
my life. The movie not only allowed me to quit teaching and
become a full-time writer but opened the door to a lucrative side
hustle as a screenwriter. And that was the least of it. The Sully
of my novel was based on my father, who was absent during
much of my young life (as Paul apparently was through much
of his son Scott's). He became interested in me when I was old
enough to occupy the barstool next to his. It was only during
the years when I returned home from college to work summer
road construction that we became close. When he died, I was
stunned by the size of the hole his absence left in my life. Still
missing his company decades after the publication of *Nobody's
Fool*, I decided to write a sequel, only to discover that I could
no longer claim sole ownership of my own fictional character.
At times it was Jimmy Russo I conjured in my mind's eye, but
other times he was Paul Newman. Even back then I suspected
what both the new autobiography and Ethan Hawke's HBO
documentary about Paul and Joanne, *The Last Movie Stars*, now
confirm: that one of the reasons Paul made such a great Sully
was the remorse he felt over his son's tragic death. After all,
Nobody's Fool is about a man who gets a second chance to be a
good father. My favorite scene in the movie isn't even in the
novel, the one where Sully and his son, Peter, are sitting quietly in Sully's pickup, the windshield thrumming rain, Sully
trying to explain why he wasn't much of a father when Peter
was growing up. Robert Benton had written a good two pages
of explanatory dialogue derived from the novel, almost all of
which Paul found unnecessary. He understood that the scene's
power lay not in articulation but its absence; that a close-up of
his face, haunted by the past, would be full and sufficient.

Though it probably shouldn't have, what did surprise me
about both the autobiography and the documentary was how

lonely Paul felt at the height of his fame. How could someone who was mobbed everywhere he went possibly feel lonely? I think the answer has something to do with the kind of fame we're talking about. I've always thought that a writer's fame is the best kind there is. Unless you're Stephen King or Margaret Atwood, people know your name but not your face. You work in solitude and, yes, that can be lonely, but every few years when a new book comes out, your name is briefly tossed around in the press, and if you're lucky you get to go on a book tour and meet some of your readers, as well as the people who sell your books. For a few short weeks you get to perform. Better yet, if you're the kind of writer who's willing to reveal something of himself on the page, the payoff is that you get to feel seen.

Movie stars, by contrast, do not work in solitude. They are always in front of the camera, always performing. Moreover, having your picture taken by a hundred cameras at once is not the same as being seen. At the height of his fame, Paul Newman may have been the most-looked-at person on the planet. What his autobiography reveals is the peculiar discomfort that derives from having millions of people view your celluloid image and, not recognizing that as a performance, imagine they've seen the real you. What Paul seems to be acknowledging in the Stern transcripts is the counterintuitive truth that the writer Olivia Laing articulates so well in *Lonely City*—that the worst kind of loneliness doesn't take place in solitude but rather in a crowd. Paul's most urgent message seems to be this: *If you knew the real me, you not only wouldn't love me, you probably wouldn't even like me.* But again, the same caveat: the fact that Paul Newman believed this to be true during a particularly dark period in his life doesn't mean it is. If anything, Paul's impulse to be honest deepened both my admiration and affection.

Since we're talking about coming clean, I'll end with a personal anecdote. At some point—in the run-up to filming *Twi-light,* I think—Paul invited Robert Benton and me to lunch at his New York apartment overlooking Central Park. He claimed he ate pretty much the same thing every day—roast chicken, a green salad and his favorite crusty bread, which he had flown in from California. The meal struck me as an odd mix of modesty and privilege. (In all of New York, there was no bakery that met his standard for crusty bread?) As we ate, the conversation turned to what we liked to cook, and when Paul expressed interest in my lobster sauce, I told him I'd be happy to send him the recipe, to which he replied—wistfully, I thought—that he would prefer an invitation to dinner. I think I understood even at the time that he was serious. I don't mean to suggest that he would've taken me up on the invitation if I had extended it. His life was far too complicated and busy to indulge many such invitations. Rather, it seemed like a good idea at the time, like something he would've enjoyed doing if things were different, if, well, he wasn't Paul Newman. The point is, I never extended the invitation. Why not? I think it's because just as Paul, even at the height of his fame, considered himself a kid from Shaker Heights, I was still a kid from a Rust Belt mill town in upstate New York, where people didn't invite movie stars to dinner. Where Paul and I met—and where we became friends—was in the make-believe world of books and movies, where men like Sully and Frank Galvin and "Fast Eddie" Felson get second chances to do things right, a world where we teach ourselves who we are and—God help us—why.

Is It Really Different?

Many people, both Black and white, are saying it feels different this time. With George Floyd's murder, white America has finally gotten its long-overdue wake-up call. And, yes, it feels different to me, too. What I'm troubled by, though, is that word *feel*. What if it feels different but isn't? Marriage vows, some would say, are merely testimony to the power of our present feelings, feelings we can't imagine will ever change. They do, though.

Since George Floyd's passing I've been haunted by an interpolated tale in Dashiell Hammett's *The Maltese Falcon*. In it, Sam Spade tells Brigid O'Shaughnessy the story of a man named Flitcraft, who disappears one day only to turn up unexpectedly in another city five years later. As she listens to the story, Brigid seems to be asking herself the same question the reader is asking: Why is Spade telling her this story in the first place, given everything else that's going on? What does Flitcraft have to do with her? Moreover, why is Hammett pausing the main narrative to tell a second tale that at first glance appears to be apropos of absolutely nothing, a story that will never be referenced again? As a puzzled Brigid listens, however, she gradually becomes more fully engaged, as if she's glimpsed Spade's purpose, which in turn signals that the reader would also do well to pay attention. Because, while the Flitcraft story may be a sidebar, a darling Hammett couldn't bring himself to kill, it might also be at the heart of everything. In other words, it might just be a parable, and not a few of these are warnings.

The story goes like this. Flitcraft is a successful realtor who lives in Tacoma with his wife and two small children. His life could not be more ordinary. One day on his way to lunch he passes an office building that's under construction, and a beam falls from a great height, nearly killing him. Stunned, he decides on the spot that he cannot return to his life because that life no longer works. It isn't that he doesn't love his wife and children or, for that matter, his work. Rather, the falling beam has "taken the lid off life" and given him a glimpse of its inner workings. To this point Flitcraft has imagined that he's in control, that his life is ordered by his choices, and in this order is its meaning. The falling beam reveals that he's not in control at all. At any moment a beam can fall, and when it does, that's it for you. You're alive today not because you've arranged things well but rather because an uncaring universe permits you to live. Tomorrow, it may not. Flitcraft has always believed that he's in step with his orderly life, with its inner workings. The falling beam proves that the opposite is true; he's actually out of step with life's reality. Solution? Walk away. Which he does.

Years later Mrs. Flitcraft hears that a man resembling her missing husband has been seen in Spokane and asks Spade to investigate. Sure enough, he finds Flitcraft living there under an alias. What most surprises Spade is how much the man's new life resembles his old one. He's back in business, though he now owns an automobile dealership. He's also remarried to a woman who, like his first wife, plays golf and bridge and trades recipes with other women like herself. He also has another young child. He has settled back, Spade explains, into the same groove he fled in Tacoma. Why? Flitcraft himself seems not to fully comprehend his own behavior, but Spade does, and he's the one who supplies the story's moral. When a beam fell, Flitcraft adjusted. When no more beams fell, he adjusted to that, too.

The more one unpacks this parable, the more discouraging it becomes and the more relevant it feels to our historical moment. For one thing, though he's had time to think about it, Flitcraft doesn't seem to grasp the significance of what's happened to him. He thinks of his first life, before the beam fell, as a series of choices that have resulted in a kind of order that pleases and comforts him. But the details of Spade's story make clear that his orderly life was always an illusion. His real estate business was made possible by a sizable inheritance from his father, and the order that he imagines he's created—the house in the suburbs, the new car in the garage, "the appurtenances of successful American living"—was already there, awaiting his arrival. The groove he slips back into so easily is in reality a kind of genetic gift. He was the man he was, Flitcraft admits, because "the people he knew were like that." It's his father's groove. His grandfather's. The order he enjoys has been created specifically to benefit people like him.

For many white Americans George Floyd's murder is the falling beam that "takes the lid off," that makes it impossible for us to see life as operating the way we once imagined. Like Flitcraft we feel that we "will never have peace again" until we adjust to this new reality. We've glimpsed the way life works for Black people and feel "impacted." The question is, how much and how lastingly, and here too the Flitcraft story is not terribly reassuring. The beam that narrowly missed Flitcraft, Spade tells Brigid, caused a chip of concrete from the sidewalk to fly up and hit him in the cheek, peeling off some skin. Years later, when Spade finds him in Spokane, Flitcraft still has the scar, which he touches "affectionately," but it's clear that he's all but forgotten it. Clearly, the fact that no more beams have fallen (near him) has allowed him to consign the experience of nearly having been killed to the farthest reaches of his memory. Nor does it seem to occur to him that there are people for whom falling beams are the rule, not the exception, and they are "impacted" by more than flying debris. Indeed, the way white people are experiencing George Floyd's death has to be fundamentally different from the way Black people are. Intellectually, we whites know that more than seventy Black people have died in police custody after having spoken the exact same words, "I can't breathe," that George Floyd spoke. And we know that in addition to George Floyd, structural racism has claimed the lives of Breonna Taylor and Ahmaud Arbery Jr. and Philando Castile and Freddie Gray and Eric Garner and Tamir Rice and Michael Brown and Trayvon Martin and so many others. But I fear that to white people it feels like *one* beam that's fallen, just as this feels like a single moment in time. It's the falling of a single beam that we need to adjust to if we're ever to have peace again. I have to believe that for Black folks it's very different. Beams have been falling on them since the first African was kidnapped and chained belowdecks on the first slave ship. Falling beams *is* their groove. I'm sure that many in the Black Lives Matter movement are pleased that so many whites have at long last joined them in their struggle, but in their place I'd be wondering if we can be trusted to stay the course. I'd love to assure them that this time is different, that we finally woke up, that there's no going back. I want desperately to believe that this is the case.

But it's not what the parable tells us is likely to happen. After all, when that beam fell, everything felt different to Flitcraft, too. To me, the most unnerving thing about the story is that Flitcraft isn't really a bad man. When he "affectionately" touches the scar on his cheek, he seems to be remembering a better self. He'd been offered an opportunity to see life for what it really is and to adjust to what he now knows to be true. Spade tells us that after the beam, he wanders for a couple years like a lost soul, as if waiting for what comes next. When he eventually slips back into his old groove, it doesn't even seem like a conscious choice. It's easy and natural—that is, in accordance with his own particular nature. And why shouldn't it be? That old groove was designed by people like him for people like him.

So, is it really different this time? It could be, right? After all, is it written somewhere that we must slip back into the grooves of our former lives? Is it written somewhere that we must adjust, as Flitcraft did, to beams not falling? I don't mean these to be rhetorical questions. Because it may, in fact, be written somewhere, in our genes, our history. But if the Flitcraft story is dispiriting, it's not despairing. Parables by their very nature have a degree of hope baked in. Why go to the trouble of telling the story in the first place if the listener can't benefit from hearing it? Sam Spade seems to have told Brigid O'Shaughnessy about Flitcraft for a reason, and while the novel isn't explicit as to its meaning (are parables ever?), we get the impression she made a grave error by not taking its caution to heart. For our purposes in the present moment the Flitcraft parable warns white people that if we're not careful, we will find peace again, that we will find comfort in structures designed with us in mind, that by slow degrees, without meaning to, we'll slip back into our old groove. If we aren't careful, five or ten years from now, when we think of George Floyd, will we affectionately touch the small scar on our cheeks and try to recapture what it felt like "when the top came off" and we glimpsed not just how America really works but our own complicity in its design?

A NOTE ABOUT THE AUTHOR

RICHARD RUSSO IS the author of ten novels, most recently *Somebody's Fool, Chances Are . . . , Everybody's Fool,* and *That Old Cape Magic;* two collections of stories; and the memoir *Elsewhere.* In 2002 he received the Pulitzer Prize for *Empire Falls,* which, like *Nobody's Fool,* won multiple awards for its screen adaptation, and in 2023 his novel *Straight Man* was adapted into the television series *Lucky Hank.* In 2017 he received France's Grand Prix de Littérature Américaine. He lives in Portland, Maine.

A NOTE ON THE TYPE

This book was set in a type called Baskerville. The face itself is a facsimile reproduction of types cast from the molds made for John Baskerville (1706–1775) from his designs. Baskerville's original face was one of the forerunners of the type style known to printers as "modern face"—a "modern" of the period A.D. 1800.

Composed by North Market Street Graphics
Lancaster, Pennsylvania

Designed by Cassandra J. Pappas